Yoga for Teens

YOGA FOR TEENS

*How to Improve Your Fitness,
Confidence, Appearance,
and Health—
and Have Fun Doing It!*

THIA LUBY

Author of the Award-Winning
Children's Book of Yoga

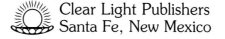
Clear Light Publishers
Santa Fe, New Mexico

Clear Light Publishers
823 Don Diego, Santa Fe, New Mexico 87501
WEB: www.clearlightbooks.com

First Edition
10 9 8 7 6 5 4 3 2

Library of Congress Cataloging-in-Publication Data

Luby, Thia, 1954–
    Yoga for teens : how to improve your fitness, confidence, appearance, and health—and have fun doing it / Thia Luby.
            p.   cm.
    Summary: Explains the philosophy and benefits of yoga to teenagers, and provides photographs and step-by-step instructions for a variety of poses.
        ISBN 1-57416-032-X (hardcover)
        1. Yoga, Hatha, for teenagers. Juvenile literature. [1. Yoga.]
    I. Title.
    RA781.7.L816   2000
    613.7'046'0835—dc21

99–41214
CIP

All photographs © Thia Luby except the following: p. 18, *Burrowing Owl* © Phyllis Greenberg, Animals, Animals; p. 32, *Flamingo* © Marianne Barcellona, Viesti Associates, Inc.; p. 34, *Pink Flamingos* © Claudia Dhimitri, Viesti Associates, Inc.; p. 38, *Verver Monkeys* © Wendy Bass, Viesti Associates, Inc.; p. 39, *Sifaka Lemur* © Tara Darling, Viesti Associates, Inc.; p. 40, *Sophie* © Carol O'Shea; p. 46, *Crocodile* © Craig Lovell, Viesti Associates, Inc.; p. 50, *Camel* © John C. Stevenson, Animals, Animals; p. 54, *Blue Chromis* © Joyce & Frank Borek, Animals, Animals; p. 60, *Honeybee* © Shay, A. OSF, Animals, Animals; p. 62, *Butterfly* © Tara Darling, Viesti Associates, Inc.; p. 66, *Monarch Caterpillar* © Carol Geake, Animals, Animals; p. 70, *Green Locust* © Austin J. Stevens, Animals, Animals; p. 72, *Locust* © Robert Maier, Animals, Animals; p. 74, *Inchworm* © Donald Specker, Animals, Animals; p. 76, *Stinkbug* © Carol O'Shea; p.78, *Praying Mantis* © Eric A. Wessman, Viesti Associates, Inc.; p. 84, *Moon* @ Marcia Keegan; p. 88, *Sioux Buffalo Hide Bow Case and Quiver*, c. 1860, photo © Marcia Keegan, Courtesy of Morning Star Gallery, Ltd.; p. 90, *Apache Hide War Shirt*, c. 1880, photo © Marcia Keegan, Courtesy of Morning Star Gallery, Ltd.; pp. 3, 85, 87, 105, *Thia Luby* © Tino Juárez

Book Interior Design/Typography/Production: Carol O'Shea
Cover Design: Marcia Keegan/Carol O'Shea
Front cover photos: © Thia Luby, © Tino Juárez; back cover photos: © Thia Luby
Film work by Rainbow Digicolor Inc., Toronto, Canada
Printed in Korea

CONTENTS

Dedication & Acknowledgments   1

Yoga and You   2
What You Need to Know
    about Yoga   2

Benefits of Yoga During the
    Teen Years   5
Yoga and Hygiene   6
Yoga and Sexuality   6
Yoga and Sports   6

The Chakras   9
Energizing the Chakras with
    Visualization   10

Getting Started   12
Warming Up   12
Your Workout   12
Deep Breathing   12
Rules for Practice Sessions   12
Ending Yoga Practice Sessions   13

Connection to the Wild
    (Animal Poses)   14
Lion Pose   15
Bird Forward Bend Pose   17
Bird Balance Pose   19
Gorilla Pose   21

Scaredy-Cat Pose   23
Happy Cat Pose   24
Cat Leg Stretch Pose   25
Bear Walks Pose   27
Bear Seated Forward Bend Pose   28
Bear Leg Lift Pose   29
Turtle Pose   31
Partner Turtle Pose   31
Easy Flamingo Pose   33
Partner Flamingo Pose   34
Flamingo Forward Bend Pose   35
Monkey Forward Bend Pose   37
Partner Monkey
    Forward Bend Pose   38
Monkey Twist Pose   39
Dog Wag Pose   41
Downward Dog Pose   42
Upward Dog Pose   43
Alligator Pose   45
Crocodile Pose   47
Beginner Camel Pose   49
Full Camel Pose   51
Swan Pose   53
Fish Pose   55
Partner Fish Pose   57
Frog Pose   59
Frog Jumps Pose   59
Basking Frog Pose   59

Connection to the Sky and Earth
    (Insect Poses)   60
  Bee Pose   61
  Butterfly Sitting Pose   63
  Butterfly Forward Bend Pose   64
  Butterfly Flying Pose   65
  Caterpillar Walking Pose   67
  Caterpillar Bending Forward Pose   68
  Caterpillar Sit-Up Pose   69
  Half Locust Pose   71
  Full Locust Pose   73
  Earthworm Pose   75
  Stinkbug Pose   77
  Praying Mantis Pose (Step l)   79
  Praying Mantis Pose (Step 2)   79

Creating Shapes
    (Strength & Courage Poses)   80
  Triangle Pose   81
  Reverse Triangle Pose   82

Half Moon Pose   85
Reverse Half Moon Pose   86
Warrior Pose I   89
Warrior Pose II   91
Warrior Pose III   92
Right Angle Pose   95

Partner Poses and Races   96
Sample Workouts   97
Summaries of Poses   99
  Basic Poses   99
  More Advanced Poses   99
  Poses to Stretch or Strengthen Specific
    Areas   100
  Poses to Alleviate Common Physical
    Ailments   101
  Poses to Alleviate Mental and Emotional
    Difficulties   102
  List of Poses According to Chakras
    Energized   103

Dedication

*This book is dedicated to my daughter
Bianca Michelle Luby
in hopes of her
continued interest in and enthusiasm for yoga
throughout her lifetime.*

Acknowledgments

I wish to thank all of the teens who appear in the photos of the yoga poses throughout this book, along with their parents for their patience and continued support.
The teens in the photos are Ali Bourguet-Vincent, Ashley Bourguet-Vincent, Brandon Casados, Kelly Hicks, Mizahn Jackson, Willie Lambert, Bianca Luby, Alex Rose, Monica Roybal, Bina Surgeon, and Alegra Yager.

Yoga and You

If you want people to admire your inner strength and beauty and enjoy being with you—

If you'd like to be stronger, more flexible, toned, and healthy—

If you'd like to feel more peaceful and happier—

Give yoga a try.

Yoga is a discipline and a science—but also a fun way to exercise your body and your mind. Some yoga poses are held statue-like, while others are very active and involve jumping movements. Doing statue-like poses will build concentration skills, physical strength, and flexibility that will help you in school or at work. The more active poses will build strong muscles for endurance and better performance in sports and other activities. When you learn how to breathe deeper and slower by practicing yoga breathing exercises, you'll feel calm and relaxed. Breathing exercises will also help you sleep better and wake up in a better mood, ready to face another day with good energy and a smile.

You can practice yoga poses by yourself, with a friend, or with a group of friends. You can practice any time of the day or evening, outdoors on the grass, or in a spacious room indoors, and you never need anything but your own body. You will be amazed at how strong you can become by practicing yoga often, and your friends will be impressed by what you can teach them.

It's important to start with the Basic Poses to begin building the strength, flexibility, and endurance that more advanced yoga requires. After you become stronger, you can begin to learn the more difficult poses. (In the back of the book you will find a list of Basic Poses and More Advanced Poses, as well as poses recommended for strengthening specific parts of the body.)

What You Need to Know About Yoga

Many forms of yoga and yogic meditation are described in the ancient writings of India, where yoga was developed over 5,000 years ago, but in this book we will focus mainly on the form known as *hatha yoga*. This type of yoga is a complete system of poses, movements, breathing, relaxation, and concentration that promotes total health and well-being—mental, physical, and spiritual. People who do hatha yoga regularly can quickly increase their physical strength, flexibility, and coordination; clear energy blocks; and develop greater mental clarity, focus, and concentration—qualities essential for success in all areas of life.

Yoga poses tone the internal organs of the body while toning muscles, keeping the muscular structure strong, and improving circulation. When you hold a pose, the circulation of blood bathes a particular area of the body to rejuvenate glands and cells, and to calm nerves.

Yoga practice focuses strongly on the brain and the spinal cord, the two principal centers of the body's nervous system. While some yoga poses are designed for energizing the body, others are aimed specifically at calming and focusing the mind. Keeping the

nerves calm and healthy is very important to maintaining a healthy mind and body. A nervous state or negative emotions like anger can have harmful physical or mental effects if these emotions and mental states occur often or last a long time. The deep breathing methods and calming poses learned in yoga ease nervous tension and help to keep your brain and nervous system working well. At the same time they help you calm your emotions and redirect energy into constructive channels.

Yogic breathing exercises produce life energy, or *prana*, which circulates through hundreds of energy channels (called *nadis*) throughout the body and clears blocked energy. The creators of yoga discovered seven energy centers, called *chakras*, running along the spine. Chakras absorb prana and send it along the energy channels to the blood, nervous system, and glands.

Each of the seven chakras affects specific glands, areas, and functions of the body. Each chakra activates a particular kind of energy that impacts our emotional, mental, and spiritual selves. If a particular part of your body feels "tight," uneasy, achy, or painful, a yoga pose can be selected to move more blood and energy into that area. With yoga poses, chakras are stimulated and energy blocks are released so that the physical stress or emotional upset can heal. Practicing yoga poses keeps the energy channels clear and the chakras open, resulting in a healthy, balanced state. (For more information on chakras, see the descriptions, chart, and exercises on pages 8 to 11.)

A person who practices yoga faithfully will eventually lose self-consciousness about his or her body and can begin to "let go of ego." According to yoga philosophy, at this point

the body is considered a fit vehicle for the soul. Although the form of yoga you will learn in this book does not involve spiritual meditations, practicing yoga poses that are calming to your body and spirit will allow you to experience a calm, peaceful, meditative state. As you continue to practice yoga, a quiet mind will emerge spontaneously and naturally. As you learn to focus your mind while holding a yoga pose, you will also improve your concentration and learning skills, and find it easier to maintain a positive mental attitude.

Yoga offers a different approach to strengthening and moving the body than sports and other types of physical activity. It gives you a chance to listen to your own body's needs by tuning in and learning which parts need direct attention for healing or strengthening. Instead of exerting energy to the point where your body feels exhausted, in doing yoga you will feel increased energy as you focus inward on proper alignment of the body while holding a pose.

Many yoga poses were inspired by animals and insects. Observing them to learn their secrets of staying strong and healthy, the creators of yoga developed a series of poses that focus on the special qualities and abilities

of different animals and insects—their strength, agility, poise, or determination. Being aware of these life forms and their qualities helps you use your powers of visualization to strengthen your practice of yoga. Some of the classical poses in this book have been renamed to make them easier to visualize. A few poses were created by the author (indicated by a † symbol in the lists at the back of the book).

When you practice yoga, you will notice that you become much more aware of your body. You will feel more alive and energized, and aware of how all the parts of your body are made to work together, in harmony. You will stand taller and be more poised, presenting a positive self-image to the world.

Yoga teaches balance of mind, body, and spirit. It is a discipline that promotes self-awareness and a strong sense of self, without overinflating the ego. Yoga is part of a system that, for centuries, has been used to build character and compassion, and is a basis for learning unconditional love of oneself and others.

Read the next sections to find out what yoga can do for you and what you need to know to get started. Then get ready to begin a new life journey through yoga. Have a great adventure!

BENEFITS OF YOGA DURING THE TEEN YEARS

During puberty and the later teen years, immense changes are taking place in the body's chemistry and physiology. The chakras are also developing and becoming more active at this time. Imbalances of the chakras, body chemistry, and physiology often show up in rebellion and mood swings. The regular practice of yoga can help you maintain balance in the different chakras and keep the spirit and soul strong and healthy, thereby benefiting both the body and mind.

According to yoga philosophy, a healthy spine creates balance and is a conduit to a sound mind. Yoga is designed to stimulate the nerves running along the spine. Poses involving twists and upside-down positions are especially effective for this purpose. When you practice all categories of yoga poses—seated, standing, lying down on your stomach or back, and upside down—you cause each vertebra (bony segment of the spine) to be slightly separated from the ones above and below it. Creating space between the vertebrae serves to "plump" the disks between them, allowing energy to flow freely to the brain and giving the blood a clear passageway to circulate in a healthy manner.

Boys and young men in their teens usually develop their legs and arms through sports or weight training. However, they often overlook flexibility of the spine, back, arms, and legs. Yoga stretching poses are highly beneficial in correcting this imbalance and in strengthening muscles that are not used in strength training. The stretching may be difficult at first, but with practice, you will become more flexible and the poses will become easier.

When a girl begins developing breasts, the muscles that hold the spine in place are often weakened or strained, because the front of the torso is carrying more weight. Doing chest opening, backward bending, forward bending, and upside-down yoga poses will strengthen arms, shoulders, and back, as well as teach these parts of your body to balance out the weight in front.

Internal organs are growing and changing during this period and can become upset with diet changes or overstimulation of nerves. Yoga helps to keep organs healthy despite everyday stresses. It also assists in balancing out the mood swings and eliminating the body aches resulting from the hormonal imbalances experienced during sexual maturing. During this growth period, yoga is useful in easing the tension of tight muscles, tendons, and ligaments, and it can also help to strengthen bones. Certain poses alleviate menstrual cramps, and others work internally on clearing energy blocks that may cause headaches, sinus problems, irritability, or digestive problems.

Yoga promotes unification of body and mind, and as you practice, it will increase your awareness and your ability to look within, think for yourself, and trust yourself. The result is that you will feel more peaceful and self-confident during a period of rapid change and be able to engage the world with a more positive outlook.

Yoga and Hygiene

In yoga philosophy, the body is considered a temple to be treated with respect, understanding, and acceptance; but dealing with the rapid physical changes of adolescence can be difficult at times. For instance, as girls undergo hormonal changes and begin to experience the internal cleansing process of the menstrual cycle, keeping the body clean and free of odor is very important. As boys undergo the hormonal changes leading to manhood, they often experience glandular secretions resulting in sweaty feet and underarms, which also require regular cleansing.

Frequent cleansing is necessary to keep the pores open so that the skin is able to release toxins freely. Bathing before practicing yoga enhances the capacity of the pores to open and expel toxins and excess oil through sweat glands. Yoga deep breathing exercises promote the process of internal cleansing by improving circulation. An added benefit of yoga practice is the release of negative energy, which can block nadis, glands, and pores.

Yoga and Sexuality

Yoga poses tone and balance the sex glands, while improving energy. During the teen years, most boys and girls become self-conscious about the changes in their bodies that go with sexual maturing. Boys may suddenly become concerned about whether hair is beginning to grow in the right places, such as on their faces or in the pubic area. They may also be concerned with muscle tone. Boys who mature more slowly or are not as physically strong as their peers often feel less manly, when they compare themselves with others. With regular practice, yoga will build muscle tone and strength and will improve energy and balance to enhance your physical performance and make your body the best it can be.

Girls experience shifting hormonal levels surrounding menstruation that can create sudden mood swings, ranging from anger to sadness. Girls also typically compare their physical changes, judging whose breasts are more developed, and worry about various other aspects of their developing bodies. Yoga practice improves fitness and health. It allows you to develop greater poise, grace, and confidence, as well as a more accepting relationship to your body and a positive image of who you are in the world.

Yoga and Sports

Throughout adolescence, when the body is still growing, and bones, muscles, tendons, and ligaments are changing, stress injuries are common. A quick or energetic body movement can sometimes cause a stress injury to any of these areas. Athletes who do not stretch enough in warming up experience injuries that often could be avoided—such as pulled hamstrings, knee injuries from tight tendons and ligaments, and shoulder, wrist, and ankle injuries from weakness in these areas. By offering a complete body workout, yoga balances out the stresses of any sport and helps correct tightness or weakness.

Stretching before and after a rigorous workout from any sport is recommended.

Sports Benefits from Yoga

Type of Pose	Primary Benefits	Poses
Seated or standing forward bend stretching poses	Strengthen and stretch the hips, legs, and Achilles tendons. Lengthen the muscles and keep the lower body more flexible.	Bear (27–9), Turtle (31), Monkey Forward Bend (37), Downward Dog (42), Butterfly (63–5)
Standing balance poses and squatting poses	Strengthen and stretch the ankles, hips, and legs.	Bird Forward Bend (17), Bird Balance (19), Bear Walks (27), Flamingo (33–5), Monkey Twist (39), Frog (59), Bee (61), Praying Mantis (79), Triangle (81–3), Half Moon (85-7), Warrior (89–92)
Forward or backward bending poses and twists	Stretch the front and back shoulder area and spine to keep the shoulders and spine loose and flexible.	Bird Forward Bend (17), Cat (23–5), Bear (27–9), Turtle (31), Flamingo (33–5), Monkey (37–9), Dog (41–3), Alligator (45), Crocodile (47), Camel (49, 51), Swan (53), Fish (55, 57), Butterfly (63–5), Praying Mantis (79), Triangle (81–3), Half Moon (85-7), Warrior I (89)
Upper body weight-bearing poses	Strengthen the wrists, arms,. and upper body.	Cat (23–5), Bear Walks (27), Dog (41–3), Half Moon (85-7), Right Angle (95)

All categories of yoga poses (standing, seated, lying down, and inverted) will balance out the lack of flexibility and strength in all areas of the body.

The Chakras

A *chakra* is a wheel or circle of energy. The seven chakras run from the base of the spine to the top of the head (crown), and each one brings different types of energy into the body. The energy wheels are thought to spin clockwise when working properly. When imbalance occurs in one or more of these energy centers, they may become sluggish and move slower or spin backward. Chakras develop in major ways as we mature spiritually, emotionally, mentally, and physically. Practicing yoga poses that balance these energy centers is the best way to keep them in good working order.

The *1st* chakra, located at the tailbone, relates to stability and independence, feelings of strength and safety, and the ability to stand up for oneself with peers and in the world at large. This chakra corresponds to the adrenal glands, which help your body and mind stay alert. Standing and seated poses work the energy down into this area for balance and order.

The *2nd* chakra, near the pubic bone, is related to the development of creative skills and also affects sexual energy. The gonads (reproductive glands) relate to this chakra. Yoga seated poses work on balancing this chakra, which can become unbalanced from the confusion of simultaneously dealing with sexual desires and impulses and social expectations and constraints.

The *3rd* chakra, the seat of the emotions, is located in the area from the navel to the bottom of the ribs, or solar plexus. It is easily agitated when emotional challenges keep nerves jangled or upset. This chakra is often over- or understimulated and is a growing and changing area deserving of attention. The pancreas corresponds to this chakra. This center must remain open and move freely so that you can remain calm and healthy. Yoga twists are excellent for working on the third chakra.

The *4th* chakra is the heart center, also a sensitive area for young people, because of the ups and downs of falling in and out of love. Opening this energy center allows you to become more loving to yourself first and then to others. This chakra corresponds to the thymus, which produces special infection-fighting cells that guard against disease. Yoga backbends open the chest and stimulate the fourth chakra.

The *5th* chakra, found at the throat, affects communication. It is easy to close off verbally when you are emotionally upset, or go in the opposite direction and say things you may be sorry for later. Balancing this chakra will help to balance out these two extremes. The thyroid, which helps regulate body growth, corresponds to this chakra. Yoga upside-down poses are useful for opening up the fifth chakra (especially Fish and Camel Poses).

The *6th* chakra, just above and between the eyes, increases knowledge and under-standing of oneself. Healthy energy flowing through this chakra strengthens the eyes, and with this, the ability to look inward as well as outward at the world with clear vision and rationality. The pituitary gland, which releases hormones to control other glands throughout the body, relates to this chakra. The pituitary is described as the "seeing" gland, the "third eye," which observes trouble elsewhere in the body and balances it out. The Lion Pose and upside-down poses—standing, seated, or lying down—stimulate this chakra.

Chakra Energy Centers

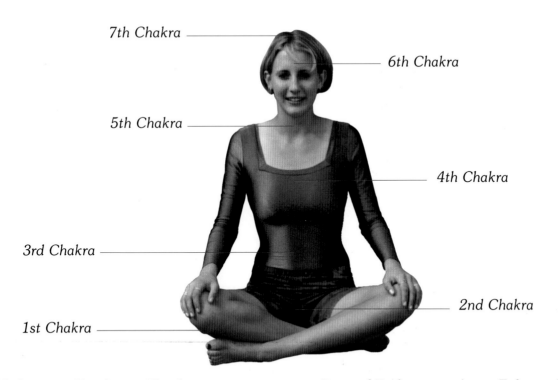

7th Chakra

6th Chakra

5th Chakra

4th Chakra

3rd Chakra

2nd Chakra

1st Chakra

Chakra	Gland	Gland Functions	Parts of Body Affected	Areas Enhanced When Chakra Energized
1st Base of spine	Adrenals	Makes hormones and chemicals (such as adrenaline) that tell the body to get ready for action.	Spinal column, kidneys	Energy grounding to the earth, physical body support, independence
2nd Sacrum	Gonads	Reproductive glands (testes and ovaries).	Pelvis, large intestine, appendix, bladder	Creativity, desire, pleasure
3rd Solar plexus	Pancreas	Produces and releases digestive juices to aid in digestion.	Digestive organs, liver, gallbladder, nervous system	Emotional centeredness, self-esteem, personal honor
4th Heart level	Thymus	Produces special infection-fighting cells.	Heart, circulatory system	Love, compassion, trust
5th Throat	Thyroid	Makes hormones that help regulate body metabolism.	Bronchial tubes, vocal cords, lungs	Communication skills, personal expression
6th Forehead	Pituitary	Releases hormones to control other glands, structures, and organs (such as the eye and optic nerve).	Lower brain, left eye, ears	Knowledge and truth
7th Crown of head	Pineal	Produces certain hormones; in the yoga philosophy, thought to be the location of the chakra that is the seat of the soul.	Upper brain, right eye	Faith and inspiration

The *7th* chakra, at the crown, or top of the head, opens up skills for discovering a higher power in the world beyond oneself. Stimulation of this chakra increases faith and inspiration and helps you to open up to the source within for guidance. The pineal gland corresponds to this chakra, which is considered the seat of the soul. When this chakra is stimulated, you can be guided into a balanced world with honor and dignity. Yoga forward bends or upside-down poses open this area, especially when the crown of the head is directly on the floor. Examples are the Fish Pose and the Bee Pose, which stimulate the senses and the brain.

Energizing the Chakras with Visualization

All yoga poses are designed to energize one or more chakras. The exercise below can be used to energize all the chakras in succession. It involves a seated yoga pose, along with visualization (meditation).

▥ Sit quietly in a cross-legged position with the spine straight. Close your eyes and focus within. Take five deep breaths to calm mind and body. Focus your attention for one minute on each chakra as described in the following steps:

▥ 1st chakra: At the base of the spine, near the tailbone, visualize a circle of red light. Try to see it spinning clockwise and feel the energy in this area. This chakra is your grounding energy to the planet, and when stimulated it creates physical and emotional stability.

▥ 2nd chakra: Near the pubic bone, visualize a circle of orange light. Try to see it spinning clockwise and feel the energy in this area. This chakra represents your sexual energy and creative skills, and it keeps your reproductive organs healthy and toned.

▥ 3rd chakra: At the solar plexus, visualize a circle of yellow light. Try to see it spinning clockwise and feel the energy in this area. This chakra is your emotional seat. When stimulated it enhances your self-esteem and keeps your digestive organs healthy and toned.

▥ 4th chakra: At the heart center, visualize a circle of green light. Try to see it spinning clockwise and feel the energy in this area. Stimulating this chakra teaches you to be more loving and compassionate and keeps your heart and circulatory system healthy and toned.

▥ 5th chakra: At the throat area, visualize a circle of blue light. Try to see it spinning clockwise and feel the energy in this area. Stimulation of this chakra builds your communication skills and keeps the bronchial area, vocal cords, and lungs healthy and toned.

▥ 6th chakra: At the "third eye," above the eyebrows, visualize a circle of blended blue and purple light. Try to see it spinning clockwise and feel the energy in this area. Stimulating this chakra increases your knowledge and understanding of truth about yourself and the world and keeps the lower brain, left eye, and ears healthy and toned.

7th chakra: At the crown of the head, visualize a circle of purple light. Try to see it spinning clockwise and feel the energy in this area. Stimulation of this chakra allows you to put your faith in a higher power, boost your inspiration to do well for yourself in the world, and keep the upper brain and right eye healthy and toned.

Now, take a deep breath and visualize the energy rising up the spine from the base chakra to the crown chakra. When you exhale, send white light down the spine, passing through each chakra, balancing and energizing them. This white light represents pure, positive energy. Let the white light slowly flow up and down the spine.

Take a deep breath, and then open the eyes and stretch out. Relax.

If it was difficult for you to imagine and stimulate one or more of the chakras, choose the yoga poses in this book that correspond to each chakra to help you stimulate and energize the ones that need work. The pertinent chakras are indicated at the end of the instructions for each yoga pose. You can also consult "Poses According to Chakras Energized" on pages 103–4.

Getting Started

Warming Up

When you are beginning to learn yoga poses, your practice sessions should be a half hour to an hour long. A yoga session—beginning or more advanced—should always start with Deep Breathing to clear tension from body and mind. After you've learned a number of poses, begin each practice session with Basic Poses to warm up each part of the body. Choose one or more poses in each category: standing, seated, lying down (front and back), and upside down.

Sample Warm-up:

(1) Deep Breathing; (2) Lion Pose and Bee Pose; (3) Frog Pose and Butterfly Sitting Pose; (4) Happy Cat Pose and Scaredy-Cat Pose; (5) Bird Balance Pose and Easy Flamingo Pose; (6) Crocodile Pose; (7) Downward Dog Pose and Monkey Forward Bend Pose.

Your Workout

As you work through the book, learning all the Basic Poses in order, keep adding new Basic Poses and continue to practice the ones you know. When you have practiced all the Basic Poses, you will be strong and flexible enough to begin working on the More Advanced Poses.

Balanced workouts for the whole body are listed on pages 97–8. The Sample Workouts include beginning, intermediate, and more advanced routines. After you've learned the poses and tried these practice routines, you may want to develop your own workout.

Deep Breathing

Begin every yoga practice session with Deep Breathing. Start by focusing on your spine as the axis or centerline of your body. Let your inhalation start in the base, near the belly, and visualize it sending energy to the upper chest. Exhale, sending the energy back down the spine to the belly. Repeat for at least 10 comfortable breaths. Breath as slowly and deeply as you can without straining.

You should practice Deep Breathing in a cross-legged sitting position until it becomes familiar. Then learn to use this breathing while practicing poses. Deep Breathing expands and strengthens the lungs and brings oxygen to the brain to help you think more clearly. Deep Breathing after you practice a yoga pose calms the nerves and releases tension.

Rules for Practice Sessions

Every time you practice yoga, be careful to follow these guidelines:

- Don't eat for at least one hour before practice.

- Do not chew gum during practice.

- Keep your feet bare to avoid slipping.

- Cooperate with your body. Never force yourself to where it hurts, but don't give up on poses that are hard for you at first. As you practice, your body will become stronger and more flexible.

- Be aware of every move you make, moving slowly and carefully while you go in and out of a pose.

- Don't worry if someone else can bend further or is stronger than you in a particular pose. Give yourself credit for what you can do now.

- During menstruation, avoid poses in which the body is upside down or the legs are held higher than the heart area.

- Before you practice a pose, close your eyes and try to see the animal, insect, or object in the same pose, and then visualize yourself practicing the pose.

- Begin by trying to hold a pose for at least one minute. If you are straining your body to hold the pose for a minute, release it sooner, and gradually build up to holding it longer. The longer you hold a pose, the more the blood pools into an area to heal stresses and release blocked energy. The stronger your body becomes through practice, the longer you will be able to hold a pose.

Ending Yoga Practice Sessions

You can use this relaxation/visualization technique after each yoga session, however long you practice. It is important to allow your body and mind to relax after working hard.

- Lie down on your back with your arms resting at your sides, palms up. Relax your shoulders. Let your feet fall out to the sides, relaxing the hips. Close your eyes and focus on your breath.

- Imagine that you are breathing through every pore of the skin. Feel your inhalations bringing positive energy into the body and mind and your exhalations releasing negative energy. You are soaking up positive energy like a sponge.

- Then imagine yourself floating in a hot air balloon in the sky, gently and freely. Float anywhere you'd like to go. Look at the blue sky and white clouds. There are many colors around you. Your balloon can be any shape and size. Float along, enjoying yourself for a few minutes, then let your balloon float down safely and softly to the ground, and focus on your breathing. Notice how slowly you breathe when you are relaxed. Your heart beats slowly when you are relaxed.

- Now let the inhalation begin in the belly, sending the energy up your spine to the crown of your head. Your exhalation sends the energy down through the feet. The body is charged with positive energy. Feel it circulating through every nadi that was cleared during your yoga practice.

- Take a deep breath, open your eyes, and begin slowly stretching your muscles. Bend your knees into your chest and roll to one side in fetal position. Then, slowly roll to the other side. Sit up slowly and notice how you feel.

Connection to the Wild
(Animal Poses)

Lion

The largest of the big cats, the lion is closely related to the tiger, leopard, snow leopard, and jaguar—the "big five" roaring cats. Though lions are native to Africa, they can survive in colder climates. The female is smaller than the male, but the lack of a mane makes her look much smaller than she really is. The lion roars more than the other big cats, to announce possession of territory.

Benefits: Strengthens the eyes, develops concentration, and releases toxins that move from the stomach up through the esophagus and settle into the mouth and tongue. This pose is a good way to relieve a sore throat and bad breath.

Lion Pose

- Sit on your heels with your hands stretched out over your knees.

- Take a deep breath through the nose, and exhale gently through the mouth, sticking the tongue way out. Look up between the eyebrows at the third eye.

- Repeat ten or more times and then rest with the mouth closed. Be careful not to hurt your throat; breathe gently.

BASIC YOGA POSE

The 5th, 6th, and 7th chakras are energized in this pose.

Bird

Birds are warm-blooded, egg-laying vertebrates with a feathered body and wings, and there are several thousand species. The developers of yoga studied the pigeon and other birds to create the bird poses. There are about 250 species of pigeons that live in all parts of the world except for the coldest regions and most remote islands. All pigeons bob their heads as they walk. With long wings and powerful muscles, they are strong, swift fliers. The pigeons that are found in cities and towns are the descendants of birds that originally nested on cliffs. When their ancestors migrated to cities, they found that the roofs of tall buildings made good nesting sites.

Bird Forward Bend Pose

▦ Squat down on the floor, open your knees wide, and bring the arms inside your legs and grab your ankles.

▦ Lengthen the spine out when you inhale. Each time you exhale, move your head further down toward the floor. Feel that stretch in your hips, back, and shoulders?

▦ After holding the pose for a while, roll the back up, release your arms, and sit down to take a deep breath.

BASIC YOGA POSE

Benefits: Relieves tension in the neck, shoulders, and upper back; stretches the hips and inner thighs; and strengthens the ankles. The blood moves into the head and down through the pelvic region for relief of headache or constipation and toning of the abdominal organs.

All chakras are energized in this pose, especially the 3rd, 4th, 5th, 6th, and 7th.

Benefits: Bird Balance Pose develops concentration and balance; strengthens the toes, ankles, legs, and upper back; and stretches the shoulders and chest.

All chakras are energized in this pose.

Bird Balance Pose

In this pose you balance as if frozen in flight.

▦ Stand with your feet under your hips. Focus on something in front of you, and balance up on your toes, leaning forward slightly, with your arms up behind your back.

▦ Hold as long as you can while breathing deeply. Work up to holding this pose longer each time.

Try counting as you hold the pose, and have a contest with a friend to see who can hold it the longest before losing your balance! The longer you hold, the stronger you will become.

BASIC YOGA POSE

Gorilla

The gorilla is the world's largest primate and one of humanity's closest relatives. The gorilla has small ears, unlike the chimpanzee. Its skin is jet black, and its hair is black to brown-gray. When walking on all fours, gorillas put their weight on their knuckles. Although they spend most of their time on the ground, they are good climbers. Gorilla youngsters are particularly fond of swinging in the trees.

Gorilla Pose

▦ Sit on your heels and place your hands in front of your knees on the floor, with the palms of your hands up

▦ Spread your fingers out and try to press each one down to the floor, while breathing deeply.

▦ Inhale while lifting your chest and straightening your arms, and exhale while pressing down through your hands.

▦ Hold the pose through a count of 15, and then turn your hands around to place your palms down, thumbs to the outside. Breathe deeply, while holding to a count of 15. Release and shake your hands out.

BASIC YOGA POSE

Benefits: Stretches the tendons running down the front and back of the forearm, and into the wrist and hand.

The 1st, 2nd, and 3rd chakras are energized in this pose.

Cat

Cats are thought to have been domesticated by the Egyptians, to whom they were sacred. They are descended from the African bush cat. Today they are familiar household members throughout the world. Cats use their whiskers to feel their way through the dark. They are graceful animals with a very flexible spine. When you spend time observing these intriguing animals, you will marvel at the many ways they turn, twist, and stretch their bodies—that's how they stay so agile.

Scaredy-Cat Pose

▥ Start on your hands and knees, then arch your back way up in the air, holding your belly tight, with your chin to your chest.

▥ Hold the pose as long as you can, while breathing deeply, for one minute or more.

You can alternate the Happy Cat and Scaredy-Cat Poses with deep breaths and faster moves. Inhale in Happy Cat and exhale in Scaredy-Cat.

BASIC YOGA POSE

Benefits: Stretches the back while strengthening the abdominal muscles. It also tones the digestive organs.

All chakras are energized in this pose.

Happy Cat Pose

- Start on your hands and knees while keeping your hands shoulder-width apart and knees hip-width apart.

- Push your belly down toward the floor and lift your chest so that you have a big downward curve in your lower back. Look up, smile, and breathe deeply while holding as long as you can, for one minute or more.

BASIC YOGA POSE

Benefits: Strengthens the lower back, hips, and legs, and stretches the chest and throat. It also tones the kidneys.

The 3rd, 4th, 5th, 6th, and 7th chakras are energized in this pose.

Cat Leg Stretch Pose

▥ Stay on your hands and knees, with your back straight and knees together. Exhale and raise your right leg way up in the air behind you, and look over your right shoulder at your foot.

▥ Inhale and lift your chest, with your arms straight, and exhale to lift your leg higher and straighter.

▥ Hold the pose for a while, breathing deeply, for one minute or more.

▥ To release, bring your leg down slowly under your hip, and repeat with the other leg.

BASIC YOGA POSE

Benefits: Stretches the front of the raised leg, belly, and arms, while also strengthening the bottom of the leg and the hip. This tones the kidneys.

All chakras are energized in this pose.

Bear

Bears are known for their heavy build, thick limbs, and powerful bodies. Polar bears' thick, cream-colored fur is an excellent camouflage, helping the bears blend in with the ice and snow in their arctic habitat. Thick hair covers the soles of the bears' feet to provide insulation and a secure grip on the ice. The only completely carnivorous bear, the polar bear survives mainly by hunting seals under the ice. They are entertaining to watch at the zoo as they swim gracefully, roll around to play, or lie down in a relaxed pose. It's interesting to see how many different poses a polar bear does as it keeps its body limber.

Bear Walks Pose

▥ From a standing position, bend down and place both hands on the floor.

▥ Now, start walking by moving your hands forward. Keeping your legs tight, move from one foot to the other in a side-to-side swing. Keep on walking to accelerate your heart rate.

▥ Then sit down and take a deep breath to relax your heart.

BASIC YOGA POSE

Benefits: Strengthens the wrists, arms, hips, legs, and heart. This pose works the blood into the head to clear the mind.

All chakras are energized in this pose.

Bear Seated Forward Bend Pose

▦ Sit down with your right leg straight out in front. Bend your left knee, placing your left foot against your inner right thigh. Keep your left foot as close to your body as you can.

▦ Inhale and stretch your arms up overhead. Exhale and bring your torso forward over your right leg, with your back straight. Keeping your front leg straight, hold your leg or your foot if you can stretch far enough. Keep your right leg tight and press it down to the floor.

▦ Breathe deeply and hold the pose as long as you can, for one minute or more, lengthening your spine when you inhale, and lowering your torso when you exhale.

▦ To release, inhale and lift your torso up with your arms overhead. Then exhale and lower your arms to the sides.

▦ Repeat with your other leg forward.

BASIC YOGA POSE

Benefits: Stretches the bent leg hip, the back of the outstretched leg, and the back and shoulders. This pose alleviates any kidney pain and brings the blood forward to tone the abdominal organs.

All chakras are energized in this pose.

Bear Leg Lift Pose

After you have practiced the Bear Seated Forward Bend Pose to stretch your back and legs, you can try this pose.

▦ Sit with your right leg out and bend your left leg, placing your foot to the inside of your right thigh.

▦ Place your hands under the back of your right knee and bend your leg.

▦ Now, try to straighten your back as you lift your right leg up straighter to flex your foot.

▦ Hold the pose as long as you can, for one minute or more, while breathing deeply. Inhale and straighten your back, exhale and straighten your right leg in the air, gradually drawing your right leg in toward your face while keeping it straight! This is a hard pose, but keep practicing and it will get easier.

▦ Release your leg slowly and repeat on the other side.

MORE ADVANCED YOGA POSE

Benefits: Strengthens the abdominal muscles and back. It stretches the back of the outstretched lifted leg and the hip on the bent leg. It also tones the abdominal organs.

All chakras are energized in this pose, especially the 1st, 2nd, and 3rd.

Turtle

Turtles are very smart creatures. When you get a chance to watch one, you will notice how they store up energy for a while before they make a move. Species include sea turtles, freshwater turtles, land turtles, and the large tortoises. Some land turtles in cold climates hibernate underground through the winter and then dig their way up through the earth to reappear in the spring. The turtle's top shell shelters its body and extends almost to the ground, making its legs appear very short.

Turtle Pose

▦ Sit down with your knees bent and your feet flat in front of your body, feet spaced wider than your hips.

▦ Try to keep your feet flat on the floor in this pose to stretch your instep (the arch), which helps flat feet.

▦ Bend your torso forward between your legs, reaching each arm under the back of each knee, palms down.

▦ Breathe deeply, lowering your head toward the floor and moving your hands back toward the hips every time you exhale.

▦ Hold the pose as long as you can, for one minute or more, and then inhale to slowly sit up and take a deep breath.

BASIC YOGA POSE

Benefits: Stretches the hips, back, shoulders, arms, and neck; strengthens the inner leg and builds the arch in the foot; and brings blood to the head to clear the mind. This also tones the abdominal organs.

All chakras are energized in this pose, especially the 3rd, 4th, 5th, 6th, and 7th.

Partner Turtle Pose

▦ Sit in Turtle Pose with another person, with your backs against each other. Extend your arms under each leg to hold the hands of your partner.

▦ Let each person pull the other's hands out to bend the torso down further. Hold the pose for a while and gradually work your head down toward the floor.

▦ Release the hands, roll your back up, sit up straight, and take a deep breath.

BASIC YOGA POSE

Benefits: Same as Turtle Pose with added stretch in the shoulders.

All chakras are energized in this pose, especially the 3rd, 4th, 5th, 6th, and 7th.

Flamingo

Flamingos are members of a family of large, brilliantly colored, aquatic birds found in lakes, lagoons, and oceanic islands off the coasts of North and South America. They normally live in tropical regions but can also be found on freezing lakes at altitudes of up to 14,000 feet in the South American highlands. Their bright pink or red plumage and their very long necks and legs make them easy to recognize. Flamingos are amazing to watch as they balance on one leg and dip their heads down to feast on small animals or microscopic plant life in the mud and shallow water.

Easy Flamingo Pose

▓ Try this Flamingo Pose to learn how much strength is involved in balancing on one leg. It may not be as easy as it looks!

▓ Stand with feet together and place your palms together in front of your chest, in prayer position.

▓ Focus on a spot in front of you, and bend forward slightly from your hips.

▓ Shift your weight to stand on your left leg and bend your right foot back toward your seat.

▓ Hold the pose as long as you can, for one minute or more, while concentrating. To release, bring your torso up, put your right leg down, and take a deep breath.

▓ Repeat on the other side.

BASIC YOGA POSE

Benefits: Strengthens the standing hip, leg, ankle, and foot; stretches the bent leg front thigh; and develops concentration and

All chakras are energized in this pose.

Partner Flamingo Pose

- Stand facing your partner with your feet together. Raise your arms in the air overhead, lean forward, and touch the hands of your partner. Make sure that you stay balanced on your own feet instead of depending on the other person to hold you up!

- Now, each of you should concentrate and bend your right foot back toward your seat and stand only on your left leg, keeping it straight. Count and see how long both of you can balance—try for one minute or more!

- To release, lower your right leg slowly and take a deep breath. Repeat on the other side.

BASIC YOGA POSE

Benefits: Strengthens ankles, legs, and hips, and stretches the arms and shoulders.

All chakras are energized in this pose.

34

Flamingo Forward Bend Pose

- This one is the most difficult flamingo pose. Be sure to practice the easy version first before attempting this pose.

- Stand with your feet together and focus on a spot in front of you. Bring your left foot up to the inside of your right thigh.

- Press your left foot into your thigh so that it doesn't slip off. Keep your right leg straight.

- Now, hold your left ankle with your left hand and raise your right arm straight up, keeping your elbow beside your ear.

- Exhale and bend forward from your hip, and draw an imaginary line toward your right foot as you bring your right hand toward the floor. If you can't reach the floor, it's okay. You can work up to that.

- Hold this pose as long as you can, for one minute or more. To release, draw that imaginary line back out to where you started, and straighten your back, standing with your arm straight up.

- Exhale and lower your arm to the side, then release the left leg. Take a deep breath. Repeat on the other side. This pose takes a lot of strength and concentration.

MORE ADVANCED YOGA POSE

Benefits: Strengthens the standing leg, hip, and ankle; stretches the upper arm and back; develops concentration; brings blood to the head to clear the mind; and brings blood to the abdominal organs to tone them.

All chakras are energized in this pose, especially the 3rd, 4th, 5th, 6th, and 7th.

Monkey

Monkeys live in tropical forests and, except for baboons and other larger primates, they mainly spend their time in trees, leaping from limb to limb to travel through the forest. There are many different species, large and small, native to various parts of the world. The macaques are common in many Asian countries and in north Africa. They have short tails or no tails. The species of monkeys found in Latin America and the Caribbean are generally small with long tails. All monkeys are agile, with flexible arms, legs, and spines.

Monkey Forward Bend Pose

▦ Stand with your feet about 3½ feet apart, toes pointing forward. While keeping your legs straight, bend over and, with your spine straight, hold your ankles and look between your legs.

▦ Hold the pose as long as you can, for one minute or more. Inhale and lengthen your spine, and exhale while lowering your head.

▦ To release, inhale and lift your back up straight. Take a deep breath.

Benefits: Stretches the backs of the legs, back, and hips, and brings blood to the heart to strengthen it and blood to the head to clear the mind. This also tones the internal organs.

All chakras are energized in this pose, especially the 3rd, 4th, 5th, 6th, and 7th.

BASIC YOGA POSE

Partner Monkey Forward Bend Pose

▥ Stand with your backs together, legs spread, and toes forward. Bend forward, grab your ankles and look through your legs.

▥ Now, grab your partner's hands in between your legs and stretch farther down. You can pull your partner's arms away to bring his or her head down further.

▥ To release, let go of your partner's hands, inhale, and roll your back up slowly. Take a deep breath.

BASIC YOGA POSE

Benefits: The same as Monkey Forward Bend Pose, adding more stretch to the arms, shoulders, and back.

All chakras are energized in this pose, especially the 3rd, 4th, 5th, 6th, and 7th.

Monkey Twist Pose

▥ Stand with the right side of your body to a wall. Squat down and bend your left arm, using your elbow to press the outside of your right knee away from the wall.

▥ Try to keep your knees together. As you press your knees away from the wall with your left elbow, rest your left hand on the wall.

▥ Extend your right arm above you from the shoulder and look up to your right hand. Feel the twist in your spine? Hold for one minute or more.

▥ To release, untwist your spine, stand, take a deep breath. Repeat on the other side.

MORE ADVANCED YOGA POSE

Benefits: Strengthens the back, hips, legs, and ankles; and stretches the arm, shoulder, and wrist. This tones the abdominal organs.

All chakras are energized in this pose, especially the 3rd.

Dog

The domesticated dog is related to the wolf and the jackal. All dogs have an acute sense of smell and hearing, and most have been bred for special purposes, such as hunting and sheepherding. They are loyal companions for as long as their owners play a dominant role in their lives. If you observe dogs, you will see how they stretch out their back and legs after resting. This stretching is instinctual. It helps dogs stay limber as they walk, run, and play.

Dog Wag Pose

You can imitate a dog looking back at its tail in this pose.

▦ Start on your hands and knees, with your hands under your shoulders and knees under your hips.

▦ Exhale and look over your right shoulder, moving your right hip (and leg) in toward your face. Breathe deeply and feel the large curve in the right side of your body. Hold the pose for five breaths, and repeat on the left side. Do the pose again on each side, holding for five breaths, or for as long as you wish.

▦ To release, straighten your back and sit down on your heels, lower your forehead to the floor, and relax your arms at your sides.

BASIC YOGA POSE

Benefits: Stretches the waist and hip, and strengthens the back and legs. This tones the kidneys.

The 3rd, 4th, and 5th chakras are energized in this pose.

Downward Dog Pose

▦ Start on your hands and knees. Flex your toes under and exhale as you lift your knees up to straighten your legs, while pressing your heels down toward the floor. Keep your arms straight, press your chest back toward your legs, and lift your seat up higher toward the ceiling. Hold the pose as long as you can, for one minute or more, while breathing deeply.

▦ To release, come down on your hands and knees slowly, sit on your heels, lower your forehead to the floor, place your arms at your sides, and relax.

BASIC YOGA POSE

All chakras are energized in this pose, especially the 4th, 5th, 6th, and 7th.

Benefits: Stretches the entire back side of the body, while also strengthening the heart and bringing blood to the head to clear the mind.

Upward Dog Pose

▥ Start in a lying down position, facing the floor (lying on your stomach).

▥ Bring your hands under your shoulders, with palms flat and fingers forward and opened wide.

▥ Inhale and push down through your hands as you lift your chest high and straighten your arms, while you move your shoulders down away from your ears.

▥ Flex your toes under and exhale as you lift your legs up from the floor. You will have a big curve in your lower back. Hold the pose as long as you can, for one minute or more, while breathing deeply. Inhale and lift your chest, and exhale and push back through your heels.

▥ To release, lower your legs to the floor and exhale as you roll your spine down slowly. Take a deep breath and relax.

MORE ADVANCED YOGA POSE

Benefits: Strengthens the lower back and front legs, and stretches the arms, chest, and front of the spine. This tones the kidneys.

The 3rd and 4th chakras are energized in this pose.

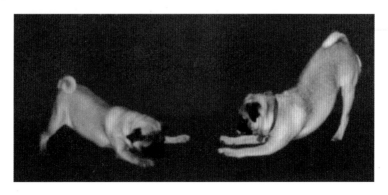

Alligator

Alligators are large lizard-like reptiles that inhabit swamps. An alligator's bottom-jaw teeth fit into pockets in the upper jaw. When its mouth is closed, you see the teeth in the upper jaw sticking out. Alligators hibernate underwater in the winter. When their environment warms up, they often crawl out of the water to catch the sun and take a look around.

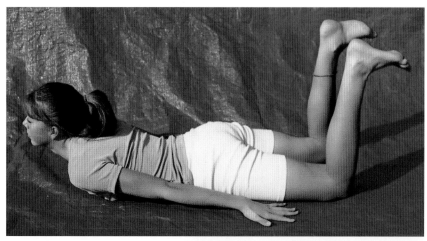

Alligator Pose

▦ Lie on your stomach and spread your legs hip-width apart. Bend your knees and bring your feet up at a right angle. Keep your chin on the floor to start, with your arms at your sides and palms down.

▦ Now, inhale and lift your head and shoulders up from the floor keeping your arms down. Breathe deeply, and when you inhale, see if you can lift your chest higher.

▦ If you are strong enough, try to lift your thighs as well, pointing the toes.

▦ Hold the pose, breathing deeply, for one minute or more.

▦ To release, lower your legs to the floor and exhale as you roll your chest down slowly. Take a deep breath and relax.

BASIC YOGA POSE

Benefits: Strengthens the back and buttocks, and stretches the upper chest, shoulders, and thighs. This tones the liver and kidneys.

The 3rd and 4th chakras are energized in this pose.

Crocodile

Crocodiles have long pointed snouts and can grow up to 20 feet long. They hatch from eggs and resemble little lizards when they are born. There are many species of crocodiles with different-sized snouts, but in most species, the fourth tooth in the lower jaw can be seen even when the mouth is closed. So, if you see a reptile and don't know if it's an alligator or crocodile, look for that visible lower-jaw tooth when the animal's mouth is closed.

Crocodile Pose

- Lie on your back with arms at your sides, with legs straight and together.

- Keep the toes of both feet pointing up and bring your left heel up and place it on top of the toes of your right foot.

- Now, twist your hips and legs over to the right side, trying to bring your left foot all the way to the floor. Both shoulders stay on the floor—you are twisting only the lower spine and legs.

- Look over your left shoulder and breathe deeply, while trying to twist farther when you exhale. Hold the pose as long as you can, for one minute or more, working on more twist each time you practice this pose.

- To release, untwist and take a deep breath. Repeat on the other side.

BASIC YOGA POSE

Benefits: Stretches the upper chest and hip, strengthens the lower back, and tones the digestive organs and lungs.

The 3rd, 4th, and 5th chakras are energized in this pose.

Camel

The two-humped Bactrian camel, like the one pictured here, is found wild in the desert highlands of central Asia. Bactrian camels and one-humped Arabian camels are both well suited to desert conditions and can go without food and water for long periods. Camels store fat in their humps and can "fuel up" on water by drinking as much as 25 gallons at a time.

Beginner Camel Pose

There are two camel poses to try in yoga. If your spine does not bend easily, practice the Beginner Camel Pose until you can easily manage the Full Camel Pose.

- Sit on your heels; place your palms on the floor under your shoulders, with fingers pointing toward your knees.

- Now, exhale and lift your seat up off your heels, while keeping your seat tight and arching your back.

- Breathe deeply, while holding the pose as long as you can. Try to stretch farther by pushing your belly up higher and resting your head back.

- To release, sit back on your heels, straighten your spine, and take a deep breath. Then, lower your forehead to the floor, place your arms at your sides, and relax.

BASIC YOGA POSE

Benefits: Stretches the throat, shoulders, chest, belly, and thighs, and strengthens the wrists and back. This tones the kidneys.

The 3rd, 4th, 5th, 6th, and 7th chakras are energized in this pose.

Benefits: Full Camel Pose stretches the throat, shoulders, chest, belly, and thighs, and strengthens the back more intensely than Beginner Camel Pose. It also tones the kidneys.

The 3rd, 4th, 5th, 6th, and 7th chakras are energized in this pose.

50

Full Camel Pose

If you want more stretch in the front of your body and a more intense backbend, try this pose.

▥ Kneel, with your knees under your hips and your spine straight.

▥ Draw your shoulders back to begin arching your upper back. Exhale and bend your lower back as far as you can while holding onto your seat.

▥ Let go of your seat and see if you can

reach back to hold your heels. Breathe deeply and hold the pose as long as you can, for one minute or more, with your head back.

▥ To release, place the hands back on your seat, inhale and lift the chest up to straighten the spine, take a deep breath, then lower your forehead to the floor, place your arms at your sides, and relax.

MORE ADVANCED YOGA POSE

Swan

A large, long-necked aquatic bird, the swan appears majestic as it glides through the water or flies with its neck outstretched. There are eight species of swans, and most are predominantly white. The species we see most frequently in the United States is the mute swan, which has a white body and black markings on the face, a long orange beak, and black legs.

Swan Pose

You can look as curved and graceful as a swan in this backward bending pose.

▓ Lie down on your stomach, with your hands under your shoulders, palms down, and fingers forward and spread wide.

▓ Spread your legs wide, inhale, and slowly lift your chest high as you straighten your arms.

▓ Bend your legs, lift your feet toward the sky, and as you slowly bend your back more, bring your head back toward your feet. Breathe deeply and hold the pose as long as you can, one minute or more, while trying to bend farther so that eventually you can touch your head to your feet.

▓ To release, lower your legs first, then exhale and roll the chest down slowly. Take a deep breath and relax.

MORE ADVANCED YOGA POSE

Benefits: Stretches the entire front of the body; strengthens the arms, wrists, and back; and tones the kidneys.

The 3rd, 4th, 5th, 6th, and 7th chakras are energized in his pose.

Fish

Many species of fish swim in large groups called schools. Smaller fish are protected when traveling in schools because a larger fish that is attempting to catch one of them may become confused upon seeing so many look-alike fish swimming together. Instead of breathing air, fish take water in through their gills and absorb the oxygen that is dissolved in the water. Most fish are streamlined and built for speed. They can move quickly using their fins (like people do when rowing a boat) and whipping their tails.

Benefits: Fish Pose stretches the throat, chest, belly, and back of the legs, and brings blood to the head, which clears the mind. It opens the lungs and tones the kidneys.

The 3rd, 4th, 5th, 6th, and 7th chakras are energized in this pose.

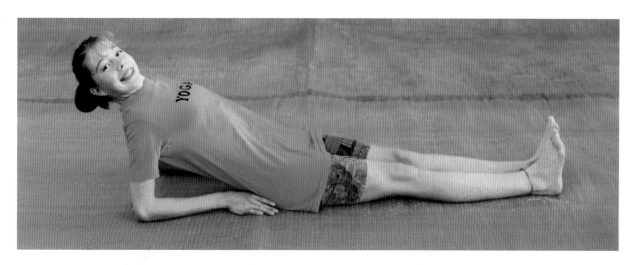

Fish Pose

▥ Sit down with your legs straight in front of you. Keep your toes up, and place your hands on the floor behind your back, with your fingers pointing forward, toward your feet.

▥ Exhale and arch your back as you come down on your elbows, with the sides of your hands resting against your seat.

▥ Push down through your elbows and hands and lift your chest higher while bending backward and bringing the crown of your head to the floor.

▥ Once your seat, legs, and head are holding the weight of your body on the floor, release your hands and bring them over your belly in prayer position, fingers pointing up. This is your fin. Breathe deeply, keeping your legs straight. Hold the pose as long as you can, one minute or more.

▥ To release, put your hands back against your seat, elbows on the floor, and slowly lower your back and head. Take a deep breath and relax.

BASIC YOGA POSE

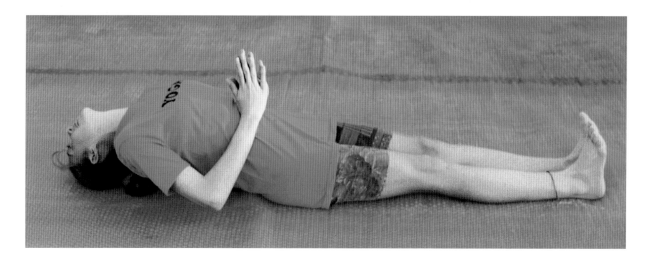

Benefits: Partner Fish Pose strengthens the back and legs, along with the same benefits of Fish Pose.

All chakras are energized in this pose.

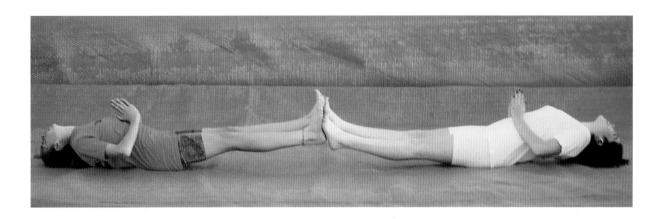

Partner Fish Pose

▦ Once you become strong enough to hold the Fish Pose, with a good, strong chest lift, you can try it with a partner.

▦ Facing your partner, sit with your legs straight out in front of you and press your feet together.

▦ Bend your back, bring your head to the floor, and make your fin with your hands. Feel yourself strong in your own Fish Pose.

▦ Once you are well balanced, press against your partner's feet and exhale to lift your legs straight up, keeping your feet together and legs tight. Lift your legs higher as you hold the pose and arch your back, while breathing deeply.

▦ Hold the pose as long as you can, for one minute or more, and then let your partner know when you are ready to release. Exhale and slowly lower your legs, and release your back as you relax.

MORE ADVANCED YOGA POSE

Frog

Frogs are small tail-less amphibians that are equally at home in water or out of it, although some species of frogs live in trees. They are powerful jumpers, able to propel themselves great distances relative to their small size. In the water, frog eggs hatch into tiny fishlike tadpoles. The tadpoles are gradually transformed into adult frogs as they lose their tails, grow legs, and develop lungs to breathe air.

All chakras are energized in this pose, especially the 1st, 2nd, and 3rd.

Frog Pose

▮ Squat down on the floor. If you cannot squat with your feet flat, open your knees and place your hands on the floor in front of you. Try to work your heels down as you hold the pose.

Frog Jumps Pose

▮ Begin in the Frog Pose and try to jump as high as you can, landing on your feet. See how high you can jump as you practice.

Benefits: Opens the hips and sacrum; strengthens the knee, front leg muscles, and ankles; and stretches the hips and Achilles tendons. The abdominal organs are toned. Frog Jumps Pose strengthens the hips, legs, and heart.

Basking Frog Pose

Frogs also like to rest on rocks and water lily pads. When you watch one resting, you can see its skin moving as it breathes.

▮ Lie down on your back, bring the soles of your feet together close to your body, with your knees open wide, and move your knees down toward the floor.

▮ Bring your arms overhead on the floor and stretch out. Keep your lower back pressed down toward the floor and breathe deeply through the belly. Inhale as you stretch your arms out and exhale as you further lower your knees.

▮ Hold the pose for a while, one minute or more, breathing deeply. To release, bring your arms down to the sides of your body and straighten your legs. Relax.

Benefits: Stretches the arms, shoulders, front body, inner thighs, and hips, and relieves tension in the belly area.

All chakras are energized in this pose.

Connection to the Sky and Earth
(Insect Poses)

Bee

Bee species are numerous; three of the most common are the honeybee (shown in the picture), bumblebee, and carpenter bee. When bees collect nectar from flowers to eat and drink, pollen from the flowers adheres to their bodies and is transferred to other flowers, thus pollinating the plants. Some farmers use bee colonies to pollinate their crops. Bees reproduce when the queen bee lays as many as 1,500 eggs per day at peak season in late spring or early summer.

Bee Pose

▦ Squat down from a standing position, with your feet hip-width apart.

▦ Spread your fingers wide. Place your index finger gently over your closed eyelid. Your middle finger rests across your nostrils, while your ring finger rests over the top of your lip and your little finger under your lip. Your thumbs can press the ears closed, while keeping the mouth closed.

▦ Make a humming sound, and feel the vibration in your mouth, throat, and chest.

▦ Hold the pose as long as you can, with your mouth closed while you hum.

▦ Open the nostrils by releasing the fingers for a moment to take a breath, and then close again to hum longer.

BASIC YOGA POSE

Benefits: Relaxes the eyes, stimulates the brain from the vibration of the hum. This pose also strengthens the ankles and legs and stretches the hips. The abdominal organs are toned.

All chakras are energized in this pose, especially the 5th, 6th, and 7th.

Butterfly

There are thousands of species of butterflies floating or hovering around trees, flowers, and grass. Most people find butterflies lovely to behold, because of their fluttering movements and wing colors, which range from very dark to intensely bright and everything in between. They seem to fly without effort, peacefully gliding through life.

Butterfly Sitting Pose

▓ Sit and bring your feet as close to your body as you can with your soles together.

▓ Hold your feet and straighten your back. Try to lift up your spine when you inhale and press your knees toward the floor when you exhale.

▓ Hold this pose as long as you can, for one minute or more, while breathing deeply. Watch to see if your knees come closer to the floor the longer you hold the pose. This action opens the hips.

▓ Release your legs and shake them out.

BASIC YOGA POSE

Benefits: Stretches the hips, ankles, back, bringing the blood down into the pelvic region to tone the reproductive organs. This pose also tones the abdominal organs.

All chakras are energized in this pose, especially the 1st, 2nd, and 3rd.

Butterfly Forward Bend Pose

▓ Begin in the Butterfly Sitting Pose.

▓ Stretch out your back and bend forward from your hips. Every time you inhale, lengthen your spine, and when you exhale, move your body forward, trying to lengthen your spine even more, and bring your head to the floor.

▓ Hold the pose as long as you can, for one minute or more, while breathing deeply.

▓ To release, inhale and lift your spine up to the Butterfly Sitting Pose, and take a deep breath. Then, stretch your legs, shake them out, and relax.

BASIC YOGA POSE

Benefits: Stretches the hips, ankles, and the back, and tones the abdominal organs.

All chakras are energized in this pose.

Butterfly Flying Pose

▥ Begin in Butterfly Sitting Pose and hold onto your big toes.

▥ Take a deep breath and sit back. When you exhale, lift both feet up from the floor, looking at one spot in front of you. Try to straighten your legs out and stretch through your heels, while keeping your back straight.

▥ Concentrate and hold the pose as long as you can, for one minute or more, while breathing deeply.

▥ Release by bringing your legs down slowly to the Butterfly Sitting Pose, and then take a deep breath and relax.

MORE ADVANCED YOGA POSE

Benefits: Strengthens the abdominal muscles and back; stretches the shoulders, hips, and inner legs; develops concentration; and tones the abdominal organs.

All chakras are energized in this pose, especially the 1st, 2nd, 3rd, and 4th.

Caterpillar

The caterpillar is the worm-like larva of a moth or butterfly. Its long, straight body is soft and is composed of many movable sections. It is interesting to watch how each section works independently to create fluid movement as the caterpillar slowly inches its way along a twig. Some caterpillars show the colors of the butterfly or moth they will become, while others will turn out completely different from their younger larval selves.

Caterpillar Walking Pose

▦ Sit on the floor and line up with at least two other people.

▦ Bend your knees, with your feet flat on the floor. Hold onto the waist of the person in front of you.

▦ Lift one hip up at a time, trying not to let go, stepping with your feet to make the line move forward or backward.

BASIC YOGA POSE

Benefits: Strengthens the legs, hips, abdominal muscles, back, and the heart.

All chakras are energized in this pose, especially the 1st, 2nd, and 3rd.

Caterpillar Bending Forward Pose

▓ Begin in Caterpillar Walking Pose , and hold still.

▓ Straighten out your legs to the sides. Keep them down on the floor with toes up.

▓ Stretch forward from your hips, straighten your back when you inhale, and stretch forward over the person in front when you exhale.

▓ When you can stretch far enough, the person in front of you can bring his or her head down to the floor, keeping the back straight. This is very hard to do, so keep practicing!

▓ Hold as long as you can, for one minute or more. To release, roll the back up to a seated position and take a deep breath.

Benefits: Stretches the inner thigh, back, and back of the leg through the heel; and tones the abdominal organs.

All chakras are energized in this pose.

BASIC YOGA POSE

Caterpillar Sit-Up Pose

▦ Begin in Caterpillar Walking Pose. Hold onto the person in front of you, with your legs stretched out wide and toes up.

▦ Keep the backs of your legs down on the floor and use your abdominal muscles to slowly roll back. Be careful not to hurt the person behind you as you lie on his or her belly.

▦ Hold the pose while breathing deeply, for one minute or more.

▦ Use your abdominal muscles to slowly roll back up to a seated position with your back straight. You can repeat the sit-ups many times.

▦ When you are finished, sit up, take a deep breath and relax.

Benefits: Lying back stretches the front of the body, and sitting up strengthens the abdominal muscles. This pose also tones the abdominal organs.

All chakras are energized in this pose, especially the 1st, 2nd, and 3rd.

BASIC YOGA POSE

Locust

Locusts are part of the grasshopper family, and like other grasshoppers they feed on grasses and other plants. In early summer, they hatch from eggs that were laid in the ground in the winter, and burrow their way to the surface. Their mating song—often heard on summer nights—is a continual clicking noise, made by rubbing their hind legs together.

Half Locust Pose

▥ Lie on your stomach, with your legs straight back. Bring your arms down to your sides, palms flat on the floor, with your fingers pointing toward your toes.

▥ Bend your elbows up to make your crooked insect legs, and press your chin and shoulders down to the floor.

▥ Now, take a deep breath. When you exhale, lift your left leg straight up in the air behind you. Try to lift it higher without twisting your back.

▥ Hold the pose as long as you can, for one minute or more, while breathing deeply.

▥ To release, exhale and bring it down slowly. Take a deep breath and repeat with your other leg. You can lift each leg several times, or hold the pose longer to build strength.

BASIC YOGA POSE

Benefits: Strengthens the back and buttock on the side of the leg lifted; stretches the front leg; and tones the liver and digestive organs.

The 1st, 2nd, 3rd, 4th and 5th chakras are energized in this pose.

Benefits: *Full Locust Pose strengthens the back, buttocks, and backs of the legs, and tones the liver and digestive organs.*

The 1st, 2nd, 3rd, 4th, and 5th chakras are energized in this pose.

Full Locust Pose

▦ Lie on your stomach, with your legs straight back. Tuck your hands under your pelvis with the thumbs together and down. Lace your fingers together.

▦ Keep your chin, arms, and shoulders on the floor.

▦ Take a deep breath. When you exhale, lift both legs up in the air behind you, while keeping your feet together. Try to lift your legs higher to lift your pelvis up off your hands.

▦ Hold your legs up as long as you can, for one minute or more, while breathing deeply.

▦ To release, lower your legs slowly, relax your arms to your sides, turn your head to one side and relax your neck. Take a deep breath.

MORE ADVANCED YOGA POSE

Earthworm

Earthworms burrow in the soil, often in the company of many of their kind. They feed on decaying organic matter, and appear above ground mainly at night, when the air is cool and moist. Their bodies are completely flexible—they can curl up and straighten out, using their entire body to move.

Earthworm Pose

▥ Lie down on the floor side by side with at least two people.

▥ Hold your body straight, with your arms overhead on the floor.

▥ Now, have someone say when to start rolling across the floor.

▥ It is important to keep your legs straight and taut so that you can roll in a straight line across the floor. Try rolling back to your starting point as well.

BASIC YOGA POSE

Benefits: Stretches the back, energizes the body and strengthens the heart. Everything is working!

All chakras are energized in this pose.

Stinkbug

Stinkbugs are hard-shelled black beetles that move slowly across the open ground as if they had nothing to fear. When threatened, they raise their hind end and squirt out an obnoxious, pungent-smelling secretion to dissuade creatures that may be tempted to eat them.

Benefits: Stinkbug Pose strengthens the back and neck; stretches the back of the legs and Achilles tendons; and tones the kidneys, thyroid, and heart.

The 3rd, 4th, and 5th chakras are energized in this pose.

Stinkbug Pose

▥ Lie face down, with your legs straight back. Lace your fingers together, and tuck your arms straight under you on the floor. Thumbs should be down, pointing toward your feet. Keep your chin, arms, and shoulders on the floor.

▥ Now, flex your toes under and start walking your feet up toward your shoulders, while lifting your seat up.

▥ Press heels down toward the floor, keeping legs straight. As your back gets stronger, you will be able to lift your seat higher.

▥ Hold the pose as long as you can, for one minute or more, while breathing deeply.

▥ To release, walk your feet back out, while slowly lowering your body. Relax!

MORE ADVANCED YOGA POSE

Praying Mantis

Related to the grasshopper, the praying mantis is a large and most unusual-looking insect. With its small triangular face and large bulging eyes, the mantis may remind you of a Hollywood alien. It eats butterflies, stinkbugs, and other insects. The praying mantis catches and holds its prey in its strong front legs, which are folded together as if the mantis is praying. The mantis is the only insect that can turn its head from side to side or up and down.

Praying Mantis Pose (Step 1)

▦ Squat down from a standing position and try to put your feet flat on the floor, keeping them together.

▦ Open your knees wide and place your palms together, as if you are praying. Let your elbows press your knees open more, as you hold the pose one minute or more, while breathing deeply.

BASIC YOGA POSE

Benefits: Stretches the hips, backs of the legs, back, and shoulders; strengthens the front of the legs and ankles; tones the abdominal organs.

All chakras are energized in this pose, especially the 1st, 2nd, and 3rd.

Praying Mantis Pose (Step 2)

▦ Once you get your knees open wide in the first step, then you can straighten out your arms in front and bring your torso down, with your head to the floor.

▦ Lengthen your back when you inhale, and move farther forward when you exhale.

▦ Hold the pose as long as you can, for one minute or more, while breathing deeply.

▦ To release, inhale, slowly lift your chest up, and then take a deep breath. Sit down and stretch out your legs, and relax.

MORE ADVANCED YOGA POSE

Benefits: Stretches the hips, backs of the legs, back, arms, and shoulders; strengthens the front of the legs and ankles; tones the abdominal organs; and brings blood to the head for relief from headache or sinus problems.

All chakras are energized in this pose, especially the 1st, 2nd, and 3rd.

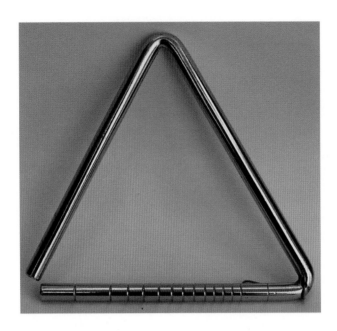

CREATING SHAPES
(STRENGTH & COURAGE POSES)

Triangle

A triangle is a geometric shape with three sides. The sides can be the same or different lengths. The percussion instrument shown here, called a triangle, is in the shape of an equilateral triangle (all sides are of equal length). When a triangle is held and hit with a wand, its vibration produces energy that creates a sweet chiming sound.

Practicing triangle poses can provide you with a similar experience of energy vibrating within the body. All chakras are energized as the spine is stretched out, with the chest and pelvis open. Energy can freely flow throughout the body. The energy charge of practicing this pose is similar to the enjoyment one experiences from listening to the varied sounds the triangle percussion instrument yields.

Notice how many triangle shapes are created by different parts of the body while holding the Triangle Pose and Reverse Triangle Pose.

Triangle Pose

▥ Stand with your legs 3½ feet apart. Keep your legs straight, feet forward, toes turned in slightly to center, and toes wide.

▥ Turn your right foot directly out to the side.

▥ Your spine should be straight, with your chest and belly forward to center. Straighten your arms out across from your shoulders.

▥ Exhale and stretch out your torso, while reaching down to hold your right leg or foot with your right hand. Keep your chest open.

▥ Inhale and draw your left arm straight up in the air. Look up to your left hand.

▥ Push down through your left heel with both legs tight and straight.

▥ Hold the pose as long as you can, for one minute or more, while breathing deeply.

▥ To release, inhale and let your left arm pull your torso up, with your legs tight.

▥ Repeat on the other side.

BASIC YOGA POSE

Benefits: Stretches the spine, hips, arms and shoulders. This strengthens the legs and ankles. It opens the chest for deeper breathing and increases balance and concentration.

All chakras all energized in this pose.

Benefits: Provides the same benefits as the Triangle Pose, but it also works into the sciatic nerve on the hip of the front leg, which runs down your buttock and leg. The twist in your mid and upper spine further strengthens your back and keeps your spine flexible.

All chakras are energized in this pose, especially the 3rd and 4th.

Reverse Triangle Pose

▦ Stand with your legs straight, 3½ feet apart.

▦ Turn your left foot directly out to the side, with toes wide.

▦ Turn your right foot 60 degrees in toward your left foot.

▦ Swing your hips and chest around toward your left leg. Hold your hips with your hands, while keeping your chest open.

- Lengthen your spine and exhale to lower your torso down as far as you can over your left leg. Keep your legs tight.

- Bring your right hand down to the inside or outside of your left foot. (Reaching to the outside of the foot is harder.)

- Inhale and swing your left arm straight up in the air, and then look up to your left hand.

- Push back through your right heel, and feel the twist in your spine. Open your chest while breathing deeply, and hold the pose as long as you can, for one minute or more. To release, untwist your spine with your hands on your hips. Inhale and lift your torso up, with your legs straight. Turn your torso and feet back to center and take a deep breath.

- Repeat on the other side.

MORE ADVANCED YOGA POSE

Half Moon

A half moon looks like the moon cut in half—a half circle. The moon orbits the Earth, and the Earth orbits the sun. At night (the time when half of the Earth, revolving on its axis, is turned away from the sun), when we see a half moon, the Earth is obstructing the sunlight so that it doesn't reach the moon's entire face. When we see a full moon, we are seeing sunlight reflected on one full side of the moon. In the "dark of the moon," we do not see any part of the moon reflecting sunlight because the Earth is moving between the moon and the sun. A new moon shows us only a crescent, or a sliver of reflected sunlight.

Half Moon Poses allow half of the body to be raised in the air at one time, while the other half holds the weight down into the Earth. The body is held both at north-south and east-west directions while holding these poses.

Benefits: Stretches the arms, shoulders, and chest, and strengthens the legs, ankles, hips, and back. This pose teaches balance and concentration.

All chakras are energized in this pose.

MORE ADVANCED YOGA POSE

Half Moon Pose

▥ Begin standing in Triangle positioning, with your right foot turned out to the side. Move into Triangle Pose, extending your torso out to the right.

▥ Bring your left arm down to the left side of your body. Look down to your right foot. Bend your right leg and place your right hand on the floor, about 6 inches in front of your little toe.

▥ Exhale and lift your left leg in the air and straighten it up and out, across from your left hip, while flexing your foot.

▥ Both legs are straight now. Keep your chest open. Inhale and raise your left arm up in the air. Try to look up to your left hand.

▥ Breathe deeply, while keeping your legs tight and holding your balance. Hold the pose as long as you can, for one minute or more.

▥ To release, bend your right leg to ease your left foot back down to the floor and hold the Triangle Pose. Then, inhale and raise your torso up, with your legs straight.

▥ Repeat on the other side.

Reverse Half Moon Pose

- Stand in Reverse Triangle positioning with your left foot out to the side, while turning your torso forward over your left leg.

- Exhale and bring your torso down with a long spine; reach for the floor with both hands.

- Bend your left leg, and then exhale and lift your right leg in the air. Your hips face down toward the floor, with your foot flexed, toes down, keep your legs straight.

- Your right hand stays on the floor about 6 inches in front of the big toe of your left foot.

- Open your chest and inhale as you extend your left arm up in the air, twisting the upper and mid spine. Look up to your left hand.

- Breathe deeply and hold the pose as long as you can, for one minute or more, with your legs strong and chest open.

- To release, untwist your torso and go back to the position shown in the first photo.

- Keep your legs strong and inhale as you lift your torso up to your starting position. Take a deep breath.

- Repeat on the other side. This is even harder than Half Moon!

MORE ADVANCED YOGA POSE

Benefits: Provides the same benefits as Half Moon Pose. Adding the twist to the spine increases flexibility, and this pose takes more leg and hip strength. It teaches incredible balance and concentration.

All chakras are energized in this pose, especially the 3rd and 4th.

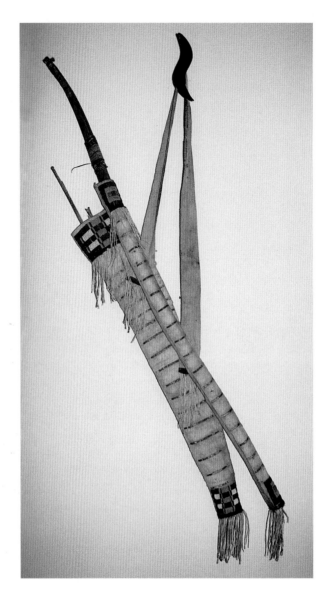

Warrior

A warrior is usually defined as a person who is engaged in or experienced in warfare. Alternatively, a warrior can be thought of as someone who is strong, courageous, and powerful. Being a warrior could be applied to any facet of life. One could be a warrior in spirit to overcome obstacles and be successful in school, business, and play.

Warrior poses build great strength and power in the entire body, but also in the mind and spirit. Holding Warrior Poses I, II, or III strengthens the legs, hips, and back. These poses also build mental strength and determination by developing balance and concentration. A person who faithfully practices warrior poses can develop a courageous soul and bright spirit.

Warrior Pose I

- Stand facing forward with your legs 3½ ft. apart and feet forward.

- Turn your right foot out to the side, with your left foot turned in 60 degrees toward the right.

- Place your hands on your hips and turn your torso over your right leg.

- Exhale and bend your right knee over your heel, while keeping your left leg straight. Push back through your left heel to the floor.

- Inhale and raise your arms straight up overhead, with palms together.

- Breathe deeply. Inhale as you reach up through your arms and exhale as you push down through both feet. Hold the pose as long as you can, for one minute or more.

- To release, exhale and bring your arms to your sides, and then straighten your right leg. Turn your torso and feet to center. Take a deep breath.

- Repeat on the other side.

BASIC YOGA POSE

Benefits: Strengthens the back, hips, and legs. This is a beginner backbend; it stretches the front of the spine, arms, chest, belly, and Achilles tendons. It tones the kidneys.

All chakras are energized in this pose, especially the 1st, 2nd, 3rd, and 4th.

Benefits: Warrior Pose II strengthens the back, hips, legs, and ankles. This stretches the shoulders, chest and arms; and opens the chest and belly so you can breathe deeper.

All chakras are energized in this pose, especially the 1st, 2nd, 3rd, and 4th.

Warrior Pose II

- Stand with your legs 3½ feet apart. Keep your feet forward, with your toes turned in slightly to center, toes wide.

- Turn your right foot directly out to the side. Your spine is straight, with your chest and belly forward to center.

- Exhale and bend your right knee, with your knee over your heel. Inhale as you lift and straighten your arms across from your shoulders. Turn your palms to the ground, and turn your head to look over your right hand.

- Hold the pose for one minute or more, while breathing deeply. Inhale as you straighten your spine, and exhale as you reach out through your fingers. Keep your left leg straight, pushing down through your left heel.

- To release, straighten your right leg, exhale, and bring your arms down to your sides, with feet forward. Take a deep breath.

- Repeat on the other side.

BASIC YOGA POSE

Warrior Pose III

▦ Begin in Warrior I position, with your right foot out to the side, torso turned over your right bent leg, and your arms straight overhead.

▦ Exhale and bend your torso forward to a tabletop position. Keep your back flat and reach out through your hands, with your palms together. Your right leg stays bent.

▦ Keeping your back flat, look over your hands to focus on one spot in front of you on the floor.

All chakras are energized in this pose.

MORE ADVANCED YOGA POSE

Benefits: Provides the same benefits as the Warrior Pose I , adding strength to the legs, back, and heart. Because balance in this pose is difficult, it develops concentration skills immensely.

▥ Exhale, then swing your left leg straight up in the air, level with your hip. Your foot is flexed, with your toes pointing down to the floor. Then straighten your right leg. Your body is in a straight line, parallel to the floor. Both legs are straight.

▥ Breathe deeply, reaching through your arms and pushing back through your left heel. Hold the pose as long as you can, for one minute or more. (This is hard to hold!)

▥ To release, bend your right leg and ease your left leg straight down, while bringing your heel to the floor, with your chest over your right leg, (1st photo position).

▥ Inhale and lift your torso back up to Warrior I position, with your arms held overhead.

▥ Exhale as you release your arms to the sides, and then turn both your feet and torso to center. Take a deep breath.

▥ Repeat on the other side; it's hard work!

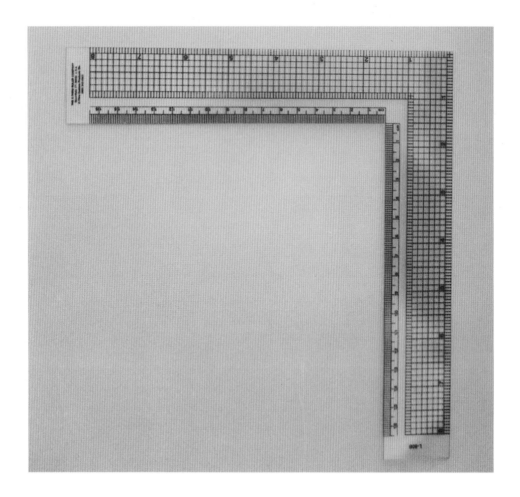

Right angle

A right angle is one-fourth of a circle, sometimes described as a 90-degree angle or turn. If you are walking east and then turn precisely to the left (north) or the right (south), you would be making a 90-degree turn.

Benefits: Right Angle Pose builds strength through your wrists, arms, shoulders, back, and legs, and brings blood to the heart and head for a clearer mind and strong heart.

All chakras are energized in this pose, especially the 3rd, 4th, 5th, 6th, and 7th.

Right Angle Pose

The Right Angle Pose allows the upper and lower body to strengthen by keeping the back and legs straight at a 90-degree angle. Great strength is required to keep your arms and legs straight. You also need concentration to push your weight through your feet into the wall so that they do not slip down.

- Start on your hands and knees, turned backward near a wall, with your toes touching the wall.

- Your palms are flat on the floor under your shoulders. Keep your fingers forward and wide with your arms straight.

- Now, flex your toes under and lift your knees up from the floor to straighten your legs.

- Exhale and place your right foot up against the wall, across from your right hip. Inhale.

- Then, exhale and bring your left foot up the wall, keeping your feet together. Your legs are straight, pushing both feet into the wall.

- Do not walk your feet up higher. Your body is held at a right angle, with your hands under your shoulders, arms straight, legs straight, and your feet across from your hips.

- Breathe deeply. Lift your tailbone up toward the ceiling, pushing your feet into the wall. Push your chest toward the wall with your back straight. Hold the pose as long as you can, for one minute or more. If holding this pose is too hard, start with your hands a little farther away from the wall until your shoulders get strong enough to hold your body at a right angle. Keep practicing! It will get easier.

- To release, walk your feet down to the floor. Bend your knees and rest back on your heels, and then bend forward until your forehead rests on the floor with your arms to the sides.

- It is important to let your head rest in a downward position after you do an upside-down pose. Relax!

MORE ADVANCED YOGA POSE

95

PARTNER POSES & RACES

Partner Poses

- Butterfly Sitting Pose, 63—With a partner, sit with your backs together and reach behind you with both arms. Stretch your shoulders and gently press your partner's knees toward the floor with your hands.

- Butterfly Flying Pose, 65—With a partner, sit with your backs together. Hold onto your own feet to open your legs and fly.

- Turtle Group Pose, 31—Sit in Turtle Pose with three or more people in a circle. Extend your arms under the legs of the people next to you and hold the hands of the person nearest you on each side. Let each person pull their partners' hands out to bring their torsos lower.

- Half Locust Pose, 71—One person lies down on his or her stomach, while raising one leg in the pose. Meanwhile, a partner helps by holding onto the raised leg to lift it higher. (Be careful not to twist the back.)

- Full Locust Pose, 73—This time a partner can help to lift both legs higher in the air.

- Praying Mantis Pose (Step 2), 79—Facing a partner in the pose stretching forward, hold onto each other's hands. Gently stretch your arms away to lengthen your back and bring your head farther down toward the floor.

- *See Also* Partner Turtle Pose (see page 31), Partner Flamingo Pose (see page 34), Partner Fish Pose (see page 57), Partner Monkey Forward Bend Pose (see page 38), Caterpillar Poses (see pages 67–9), Earthworm Pose (see page 75).

Races Using the Poses

- Bear Walks Race—Line up side by side with two or more people in Bear Walks Pose (27). Have someone positioned ahead at a finish line to say "start" to begin the race. Keep your legs straight so that you can walk swinging your legs side to side, while using your hands and feet to get to the finish line.

- Turtle Race—Line up side by side with two or more people in Turtle Pose (31). Have someone positioned ahead at a finish line to say "start" to begin the race. Hold onto your ankles and lift one hip up at a time to step ahead to the finish line.

- Frog Race—Line up side by side with two or more people in Frog Pose (59). Have someone positioned ahead at a finish line to say "start" to begin the race. Jump like a frog on your feet to the finish line.

- Caterpillar Race—Start with four or more people in Caterpillar Walking Pose (67) to create two lines. Line up the caterpillars side by side. Have someone positioned ahead at a finish line to say "start" to begin the race. Hold onto the person in front of you, and lift one hip up at a time to step ahead without letting go until you reach the finish line. Try this race backwards too!

Sample Workouts

In doing a yoga workout, try to hold each pose one minute or longer. Repeating the pose will allow the body to become more familiar with the pose, and to stretch and strengthen further. Basic Yoga Workouts like those below are designed to be practiced in about a half hour, depending on how long you are able to hold the poses and whether you decide to repeat them.

Basic Yoga Session I
(about ½ hour)

Deep Breathing (10 breaths), 12
Lion Pose, 15
Monkey Forward Bend Pose, 37
Gorilla Pose, 21
Scaredy-Cat Pose, 23
Happy Cat Pose, 24
Cat Leg Stretch Pose, 25
Bird Forward Bend Pose, 17
Bear Seated Forward Bend Pose, 28
Butterfly Sitting Pose, 63
Downward Dog Pose, 42
Triangle Pose, 81
Easy Flamingo Pose, 33
Alligator Pose, 45
Beginner Camel Pose, 49
Crocodile Pose, 47
Basking Frog Pose, 59
Relaxation

Basic Yoga Session II
(about ½ hour)

Deep Breathing (10 breaths), 12
Bee Pose, 61
Bird Balance Pose, 19
Gorilla Pose, 21
Monkey Forward Bend Pose, 37
Bear Walks Pose, 27
Praying Mantis Pose (Step 1), 79
Triangle Pose, 81
Warrior Pose I, 89
Warrior Pose II, 91
Half Locust Pose, 71
Beginner Camel Pose, 49
Downward Dog Pose, 42
Crocodile Pose, 47
Fish Pose, 55
Basking Frog Pose, 59
Relaxation

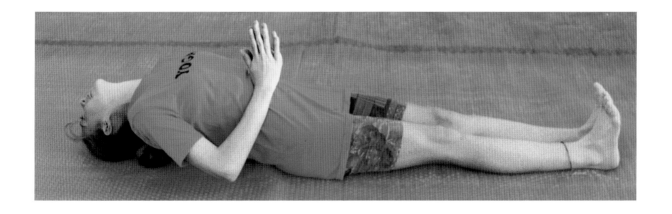

Intermediate Yoga Session
(1 hour or longer)

Deep Breathing
  (10 breaths), 12
Lion Pose, 15
Earthworm Pose, 75
Scaredy-Cat Pose, 23
Happy Cat Pose, 24
Cat Leg Stretch Pose, 25
Butterfly Sitting Pose, 63
Butterfly Forward Bend Pose,
  64
Praying Mantis Pose
  (Step 1), 79
* Praying Mantis Pose
  (Step 2), 79
Bear Seated Forward
  Bend Pose, 28
* Bear Leg Lift Pose, 29
Triangle Pose, 81
* Reverse Triangle Pose, 82–3
Monkey Forward Bend Pose,
  37
Partner Monkey Forward
  Bend Pose, 38
Partner Flamingo Pose, 34
* Flamingo Forward Bend Pose,
  35
Half Locust Pose, 71
* Full Locust Pose, 73
Gorilla Pose, 21
Beginner Camel Pose, 49
* Full Camel Pose, 51
Dog Wag Pose, 41
Downward Dog Pose, 42
* Upward Dog Pose, 43
* Right Angle Pose, 95
Basking Frog Pose, 59
Relaxation

Intermediate Yoga Session
(1 hour or longer)

Deep Breathing
  (10 breaths), 12
Bee Pose, 61
Caterpillar Walking Pose, 67
Caterpillar Bending Pose, 68
Caterpillar Sit-Up Pose, 69
Butterfly Sitting Pose, 63
Butterfly Forward Bend Pose,
  64
* Butterfly Flying Pose, 65
Gorilla Pose, 21
Triangle Pose, 81
* Reverse Triangle Pose, 82–3
* Half Moon Pose, 85
Warrior Pose I, 89
Warrior Pose II, 91
* Stinkbug Pose, 77
Downward Dog Pose, 42
* Upward Dog Pose, 43
* Swan Pose, 53
* Monkey Twist Pose, 39
Praying Mantis Pose
  Step 1), 79
* Praying Mantis Pose
  (Step 2), 79
* Right Angle Pose, 95
Fish Pose, 55
* Partner Fish Pose, 57
Basking Frog Pose, 59
Relaxation

More Advanced Yoga Session
(1 hour or longer)

Deep Breathing
  (10 breaths), 12
Lion Pose, 15
Gorilla Pose, 21
Butterfly Sitting Pose, 63
Butterfly Forward Bend Pose,
  64
* Butterfly Flying Pose, 65
Downward Dog Pose, 42
* Upward Dog Pose, 43
Bear Seated Forward Bend
  Pose, 28
* Bear Leg Lift Pose, 29
Monkey Forward Bend Pose,
  37
Praying Mantis Pose
  (Step 1), 79
* Praying Mantis Pose
  (Step 2), 79
Triangle Pose, 81
* Reverse Triangle Pose, 82–3
* Half Moon Pose, 85
* Reverse Half Moon Pose,
  86–7
Warrior Pose I, 89
Warrior Pose II, 91
* Warrior Pose III, 92
* Stinkbug Pose, 77
Half Locust Pose, 71
* Full Locust Pose, 73
* Full Camel Pose, 51
* Swan Pose, 53
Fish Pose, 55
* Partner Fish Pose, 57
* Right Angle Pose, 95
Basking Frog Pose, 59
Relaxation

*** More Advanced Poses**

Summaries of Poses

Basic Poses

The following are the Basic Poses you should learn. They are the foundation on which you build and develop balance, concentration, flexibility, and strength. Once you have mastered these poses, you can move on to the More Advanced Poses. Use the Basic Poses to warm up, even if you are able to practice the more difficult ones. The list follows the order of poses presented in the sections on animal, insect, and shape poses. They flow in a sequence to reach every part of the body in a balanced manner.

Lion Pose, 15
Bird Forward Bend Pose, 17
Bird Balance Pose, 19
Gorilla Pose, 21
Scaredy-Cat Pose, 23
Happy Cat Pose, 24
Cat Leg Stretch Pose, 25
Bear Walks Pose, 27
Bear Seated Forward Bend Pose, 28
Turtle Pose, 31
Partner Turtle Pose, 31
Easy Flamingo Pose, 33
Partner Flamingo Pose, 34
Monkey Forward Bend Pose, 37
Partner Monkey Forward Bend Pose, 38
Dog Wag Pose, 41
Downward Dog Pose, 42
Alligator Pose, 45
Crocodile Pose, 47
Beginner Camel Pose, 49
Fish Pose, 55
Frog Pose, 59
Frog Jumps Pose, 59
Basking Frog Pose, 59

Bee Pose, 61
Butterfly Sitting Pose, 63
Butterfly Forward Bend Pose, 64
Caterpillar Walking Pose, 67
Caterpillar Bending Forward Pose, 68
Caterpillar Sit-Up Pose, 69
Half Locust Pose, 71
Earthworm Pose, 75
Praying Mantis Pose (Step 1), 79
Triangle Pose, 81
Warrior Pose I, 89
Warrior Pose II, 91

More Advanced Poses

After you have practiced a variety of the basic poses to build flexibility, strength, and balance, you may be ready to try some of the more difficult poses.

Bear Leg Lift Pose, 29
Flamingo Forward Bend Pose, 35
Monkey Twist Pose, 39
Upward Dog Pose, 43
Full Camel Pose, 51
Swan Pose, 53
Partner Fish Pose, 57
Butterfly Flying Pose, 65
Full Locust Pose, 73
Stinkbug Pose, 77
Praying Mantis Pose (Step 2), 79
Reverse Triangle Pose, 82–3
Half Moon Pose, 85
Reverse Half Moon Pose, 86-7
Warrior Pose III, 92
Right Angle Pose, 95

Poses to Stretch or Strengthen Specific Areas

A good way to set up a yoga routine is to choose one or more poses from each of these categories to practice in one session. You can pick different poses from each category to try on different days. Again, the poses are listed in the order they appear in the sections on animal, insect, and shape poses. Poses requiring one or all of the following—great strength, balance, and concentration—are marked with an asterisk (*). Practice these once you have mastered other poses.

Hip and Back Stretching Poses

Bird Forward Bend Pose, 17
Scaredy-Cat Pose, 23
Happy Cat Pose, 24
Cat Leg Stretch Pose, 25
Bear Seated Forward Bend Pose, 28
Turtle Pose, 31
Partner Turtle Pose, 31
* Flamingo Forward Bend Pose, 35
Monkey Forward Bend Pose, 37
Partner Monkey Forward Bend Pose, 38
* Monkey Twist Pose, 39
Dog Wag Pose, 41
Downward Dog Pose, 42
Frog Pose, 59
Bee Pose, 61
Butterfly Sitting Pose, 63
Butterfly Forward Bend Pose, 64
Caterpillar Bending Forward Pose, 68
Earthworm Pose, 75
Praying Mantis Poses, 79
Triangle Pose, 81
* Reverse Triangle Pose, 82-3
* Half Moon Pose, 85
Warrior Pose II, 91
* Warrior Pose III, 92–3
* Right Angle Pose, 95

Inner Thigh and Hip Opening and Stretching Poses

Bird Forward Bend Pose, 17
Bear Seated Forward Bend Pose, 28

* Bear Leg Lift Pose, 29
Turtle Pose, 31
Partner Turtle Pose, 31
Frog Pose, 59
Basking Frog Pose, 59
Butterfly Sitting Pose, 63
Butterfly Forward Bend Pose, 64
* Butterfly Flying Pose, 65
Caterpillar Walking Pose, 67
Caterpillar Bending Forward Pose, 68
Caterpillar Sit-Up Pose, 69
Praying Mantis Poses, 79
Triangle Pose, 81
* Half Moon Pose, 85
Warrior Pose II, 91

Shoulder and Chest Opening Poses

Happy Cat Pose, 24
* Monkey Twist Pose, 39
Alligator Pose, 45
Beginner Camel Pose, 49
* Full Camel Pose, 51
* Swan Pose, 53
Fish Pose, 55
* Partner Fish Pose, 57
* Butterfly Flying Pose, 65
Triangle Pose, 81
* Reverse Triangle Pose, 82–3
* Half Moon Pose, 85
* Reverse Half Moon Pose, 86–7
Warrior Pose II, 91

Wrist Stretching Exercises

Gorilla Pose, 21
* Monkey Twist Pose, 39

Balance Poses

Bird Balance Pose, 19
Cat Leg Stretch Pose, 25
Easy Flamingo Pose, 33
Partner Flamingo Pose, 34
* Flamingo Forward Bend Pose, 35
* Butterfly Flying Pose, 65
Triangle Pose, 81
* Reverse Triangle Pose, 82–3
* Half Moon Pose, 85
* Reverse Half Moon Pose, 86–7
* Warrior Pose III, 92–3
* Right Angle Pose, 95

Back Strengthening Poses

Scaredy-Cat Pose, 23
Happy Cat Pose, 24
Cat Leg Stretch Pose, 25
* Bear Leg Lift Pose, 29
* Upward Dog Pose, 43
Alligator Pose, 45
Crocodile Pose, 47
Beginner Camel Pose, 49
* Full Camel Pose, 51
* Swan Pose, 53
Fish Pose, 55
* Partner Fish Pose, 57
* Butterfly Flying Pose, 65
Half Locust Pose, 71
* Full Locust Pose, 73
* Stinkbug Pose, 77
* Reverse Triangle Pose, 82–3
* Reverse Half Moon Pose, 86–7
Warrior Pose I, 89
* Right Angle Pose, 95

* More Advanced Poses

Abdominal Strengthening Poses

Bird Forward Bend Pose, 17
Bird Balance Pose, 19
Scaredy-Cat Pose, 23
Bear Seated Forward Bend
   Pose, 28
* Bear Leg Lift Pose, 29
Turtle Pose, 31
Partner Turtle Pose, 31
* Flamingo Forward Bend Pose,
   35
Monkey Forward Bend Pose, 37
Partner Monkey Forward Bend
   Pose, 38
* Monkey Twist Pose, 39
Dog Wag Pose, 41
Crocodile Pose, 47
* Butterfly Flying Pose, 65
Caterpillar Sit-Up Pose, 69
* Praying Mantis Pose
   (Step 2), 79
* Reverse Triangle Pose, 82–3
* Reverse Half Moon Pose, 86–7
* Warrior Pose III, 92–3

Spinal Twist Poses

* Monkey Twist Pose, 39
Crocodile Pose, 47
* Reverse Triangle Pose, 82
* Reverse Half Moon Pose, 86

Spine Bending Poses

Scaredy-Cat Pose, 23
Happy Cat Pose, 24
Turtle Pose, 31
* Upward Dog Pose, 43
Alligator Pose, 45
Beginner Camel Pose, 49
* Full Camel Pose, 51
* Swan Pose, 53
* Fish Poses, 55, 57

Upper Body Strengthening Poses

Bear Walks Pose, 27
* Monkey Twist Pose, 39
Downward Dog Pose, 42
* Upward Dog Pose, 43
* Right Angle Pose, 95

Ankle, Leg, and Hip Strengthening Poses

Bird Forward Bend Pose, 17
Bird Balance Pose, 19
Cat Leg Stretch Pose, 25
Easy Flamingo pose, 33
Partner Flamingo Pose, 34
* Flamingo Forward Bend Pose,
   35
Monkey Forward Bend Pose, 37
Partner Monkey Forward Bend
   Pose, 38
* Monkey Twist Pose, 39
Frog Pose, 59
Frog Jumps Pose, 59,
Bee Pose, 61
Caterpillar Walking Pose, 67
Praying Mantis Poses, 79
Triangle Pose, 81
* Reverse Triangle Pose, 82–3
* Half Moon Pose, 85
* Reverse Half Moon Pose, 86–7
Warrior Pose I, 89
Warrior Pose II, 91
* Warrior Pose III, 92–3
* Right Angle Pose, 95

Poses to Alleviate Common Physical Ailments

Yoga can help relieve physical ailments. Holding a pose allows the blood to work into specific areas of the body to tone internal organs and release stress. Be sure that you hold the pose one or two minutes. More Advanced Poses are marked with an asterisk (*)

Lower Back Ache
Scaredy Cat Pose, 23
Cat Leg Stretch Pose, 25
Dog Wag Pose, 41
Downward Dog Pose, 42
Triangle Pose, 81
* Reverse Triangle Pose, 82-3

Colds or Sinus Problems
(Deep Breathing, 12)
Turtle Pose, 31
* Flamingo Forward Bend Pose, 35
Monkey Forward Bend Pose, 37
Downward Dog Pose, 42
Fish Pose, 55
* Right Angle Pose, 95

Headache
(Deep Breathing, 12)
Bear Seated Forward Bend
   Pose, 28
Monkey Forward Bend Pose, 37
Downward Dog Pose, 42
* Right Angle Pose, 95

Indigestion
Bear Seated Forward Bend
   Pose, 28
Alligator Pose, 45
Crocodile Pose, 47
Basking Frog Pose, 59

Constipation
Bear Seated Forward Bend
   Pose, 28
* Flamingo Forward Bend Pose,
   35
Monkey Forward Bend Pose, 37
* Monkey Twist Pose, 39
Frog Pose, 59
Crocodile Pose, 47

Menstrual Cramps
Beginner Camel Pose, 49
Basking Frog Pose, 59
Butterfly Sitting Pose, 63
Fetal Position

Poses to Alleviate Emotional and Mental Difficulties

Sadness
Open the 3rd chakra, which rules the emotions, through poses that stimulate the belly. Try the following:
Scaredy-Cat Pose, 23
Happy Cat Pose, 24
Crocodile Pose, 47
Fish Pose, 55
Warrior Pose I, 89
Warrior Pose II, 91

Difficulty sharing with or loving others
If you are fighting with people and having trouble getting along, work on poses that stimulate and open the 4th chakra, which allows the heart to open for love and compassion. Try the following:
Bird Forward Bend Pose, 17
Turtle Pose, 31
Alligator Pose, 45
Beginner Camel Pose, 49
* Swan Pose, 53
Fish Pose, 55
* Full Camel Pose, 51
* Praying Mantis Pose (Step 2), 79

Sluggishness or slow thinking
If you are having a hard time waking up or thinking clearly, try opening the 6th and 7th chakras, which stimulate the mind and open passageways to the brain. Try the following:
Bear Walks Pose, 27
* Flamingo Forward Bend Pose, 35
Monkey Forward Bend Pose, 37
Downward Dog Pose, 42
Fish Pose, 55
* Right Angle Pose, 95

Difficulties in maintaining balance
If you have difficulty being grounded, that is, you feel clumsy because you are tripping, spilling things, or falling, your mind needs to focus for concentration. You need to work on the 1st chakra, which sends the energy downward into your feet for balance. Try standing balance poses, such as the following:
Bird Balance Pose, 19
Easy Flamingo Pose, 33
Partner Flamingo Pose, 34
* Flamingo Forward Bend Pose, 35
Triangle Pose, 81

* Reverse Triangle Pose, 82-3
* Half Moon Pose, 85
* Reverse Half Moon Pose, 86–7
Warrior Pose I, 89
Warrior Pose II, 91
* Warrior Pose III, 92–3

Nervous tension
If you feel too wound up and wish to calm down, try the following:
Basking Frog Pose, 59
Chakra Visualization, 10–11
Deep Breathing, 12
Relax in Fetal Position

***More Advanced Poses**

List of Poses According to Chakras Energized

All Chakras

Bird Forward Bend Pose (especially 3rd, 4th, 5th, 6th, and 7th), 17
Bird Balance Pose, 19
Scaredy-Cat Pose, 23
Cat Leg Stretch Pose, 25
Bear Walks Pose, 27
Bear Seated Forward Bend Pose, 28
Bear Leg Lift Pose (especially 1st, 2nd, and 3rd), 29
Turtle and Partner Turtle Poses (especially 3rd, 4th, 5th, 6th, and 7th), 31
Easy Flamingo Pose, 33
† Partner Flamingo Pose, 33
Flamingo Forward Bend Pose (especially 3rd, 4th, 5th, 6th, and 7th), 35
Monkey Forward Bend Pose (especially 3rd, 4th, 5th, 6th, and 7th), 37
Partner Monkey Forward Bend Pose (especially 3rd, 4th, 5th, 6th, and 7th), 38
† Monkey Twist Pose (especially 3rd), 39
Downward Dog Pose (especially 4th, 5th, 6th, and 7th), 42
† Partner Fish Pose, 57
Frog Pose (especially 1st, 2nd, and 3rd), 59
Basking Frog Pose, 59
Bee Pose (especially 5th, 6th, and 7th), 61
Butterfly Sitting Pose (especially 1st, 2nd, and 3rd), 63
Butterfly Forward Bend Pose, 64
Butterfly Flying Pose (especially 1st, 2nd, 3rd, and 4th), 65
† Caterpillar Walking Pose, (especially 1st, 2nd, and 3rd), 68

† Caterpillar Bending Forward Pose, 68
† Caterpillar Sit-Up Pose (especially 1st, 2nd, and 3rd), 69
Earthworm Pose, 75
Praying Mantis Pose (Steps 1 and 2) (especially 1st, 2nd, and 3rd), 79
Triangle Pose, 81
Reverse Triangle Pose (especially 3rd and 4th), 82–3
Half Moon Pose, 85
Reverse Half Moon Pose (especially 3rd and 4th), 86–7
Warrior Pose I (especially 1st, 2nd, 3rd, and 4th), 89
Warrior Pose II (especially 1st, 2nd, 3rd, and 4th), 91
Warrior Pose III, 92–3
Right Angle Pose (especially 3rd, 4th, 5th, 6th, and 7th), 95

1st Chakra

Gorilla Pose, 21
Bear Leg Lift Pose, 29
Frog Pose, 59
Butterfly Sitting Pose, 63
Butterfly Flying Pose, 65
† Caterpillar Walking Pose, 67
† Caterpillar Sit-Up Pose, 69
Half Locust Pose, 71
Full Locust Pose, 73
Praying Mantis Pose, 79
Warrior Pose I, 89
Warrior Pose II, 91
Warrior Pose III, 93

2nd Chakra

Gorilla Pose, 21
Bear Leg Lift Pose, 29
Frog Pose, 59
Butterfly Sitting Pose, 63
Butterfly Flying Pose, 65

† Caterpillar Walking Pose, 67
† Caterpillar Sit-Up Pose, 69
Half Locust Pose, 71
Full Locust Pose, 73
Praying Mantis Poses, 79
Warrior Pose I, 89
Warrior Pose II, 91

3rd Chakra

Bird Forward Bend Pose, 17
Gorilla Pose, 21
Happy Cat Pose, 24
Bear Leg Lift Pose, 29
Turtle and Partner Turtle Poses, 31
Flamingo Forward Bend Pose, 35
Monkey Forward Bend Pose, 37
Partner Monkey Forward Bend Pose, 38
† Monkey Twist Pose, 39
Dog Wag Pose, 41
Upward Dog Pose, 43
Alligator Pose, 45
Crocodile Pose, 47
Beginner Camel Pose, 49
Full Camel Pose, 51
Swan Pose, 53
Fish Pose, 55
Frog Pose, 59
Butterfly Sitting Pose, 63
Butterfly Flying Pose, 65
† Caterpillar Walking Pose, 67
† Caterpillar Sit-Up Pose, 69
Half Locust Pose, 71
Full Locust Pose, 73
† Stinkbug Pose, 77
Praying Mantis Poses, 79
Reverse Triangle Pose, 82–3
Reverse Half Moon Pose, 86–7
Warrior Pose I, 89
Warrior Pose II, 91
Right Angle Pose, 95

† Poses created by the author

4th Chakra

Bird Forward Bend Pose, 17
Happy Cat Pose, 24
Turtle and Partner Turtle Poses,
    31
Flamingo Forward Bend Pose,
    35
Monkey Forward Bend Pose, 37
Partner Monkey Forward Bend
    Pose, 38
Dog Wag Pose, 41
Downward Dog Pose, 42
Upward Dog Pose, 43
Alligator Pose, 45
Crocodile Pose, 47
Beginner Camel Pose, 49
Full Camel Pose, 51
Swan Pose, 53
Fish Pose, 55
Butterfly Flying Pose, 65
Half Locust Pose, 71
Full Locust Pose, 73
† Stinkbug Pose, 77
Reverse Triangle Pose, 82–3
Reverse Half Moon Pose, 86–7
Warrior Pose I, 89
Warrior Pose II, 91
Right Angle Pose, 95

5th Chakra

Lion Pose, 15
Bird Forward Bend Pose, 17
Happy Cat Pose, 23
Turtle and Partner Turtle Poses,
    31
Flamingo Forward Bend Pose,
    35
Monkey Forward Bend Pose, 37
Partner Monkey Forward Bend
    Pose, 38
Dog Wag Pose, 41
Downward Dog Pose, 42
Crocodile Pose, 47
Beginner Camel Pose, 49
Full Camel Pose, 51
Swan Pose, 53

Fish Pose, 55
Bee Pose, 61
Half Locust Pose, 71
Full Locust Pose, 73
† Stinkbug Pose, 77
Right Angle Pose, 95

6th Chakra

Lion Pose, 15
Bird Forward Bend Pose, 17
Happy Cat Pose, 24
Turtle and Partner Turtle Poses,
    31
Flamingo Forward Bend Pose,
    35
Monkey Forward Bend Pose, 37
Partner Monkey Forward Bend
    Pose, 38
Downward Dog Pose, 42
Beginner Camel Pose, 49
Full Camel Pose, 51
Swan Pose, 53

Fish Pose, 55
Bee Pose, 61
Right Angle Pose, 95

7th Chakra

Lion Pose, 15
Bird Forward Bend Pose, 17
Happy Cat Pose, 24
Turtle and Partner Turtle Poses,
    31
Flamingo Forward Bend Pose,
    35
Monkey Forward Bend Pose, 37
Partner Monkey Forward Bend
    Pose, 38
Downward Dog Pose, 42
Beginner Camel Pose, 49
Full Camel Pose, 51
Swan Pose, 53
Fish Pose, 55
Bee Pose, 61
Right Angle Pose, 95

† *Poses created by the author*

About the Author

Thia Luby has studied both the physical practice and philosophy of yoga for more than 25 years and has been teaching yoga in Santa Fe, New Mexico, since 1978. She has developed yoga programs for children, teenagers, and adults, and teaches yoga to teenagers in high schools and treatment centers. She has created a nationally distributed adult audio tape and children's video on yoga. Luby's innovative program for children is presented in her book, *Children's Book of Yoga*, published by Clear Light Publishers and selected by *School Library Journal* as one of the best children's books.